PROFESSIONAL IMPRESSIONS

Etiquette for Everyone, Every Day

Marjorie Brody, MA, CSP, CMC

Books by Marjorie Brody, MA, CSP, CMC

21st Century Pocket Guides to Proper Business Protocol (four-booklet series)

Speaking is an Audience-Centered Sport

Speaking Your Way to the Top: Making Powerful Business Presentations

21 Ways to Springboard Your Speaking, Training & Consulting Career

Power Marketing For Consultants (with Allen D'Angelo, Bill Kerley and Bernard Zick)

Complete Business Etiquette Handbook

Business Etiquette

Minding Your Business Manners

Climbing the Corporate Ladder

Power Presentations

Professional Impressions
Etiquette For Everyone, Every Day

Marjorie Brody, MA, CSP, CMC

Copy Editors: Miryam S. Roddy & June Fox

Cover Design & Cartoons: The Cartoon Resource

Published by Career Skills Press
815 Greenwood Avenue, Suite 8
Jenkintown, PA 19046 USA
800-726-7936
Tel: 215-886-1688
Fax: 215-886-1699
E-mail: brody@BrodyCommunications.com
Web: www.BrodyCommunications.com
www.marjoriebrody.com

Library of Congress Cataloging-in-Publication Data in Process

ISBN: 0-965-4827-4-X

ACKNOWLEDGEMENTS

Lots of acknowledgements are in order for this book.

For his patience, my husband, Dr. Alan Frieman
For supporting me on a daily basis, the staff of Brody
    Communications Ltd.
For sharing their experiences, my clients
For editing and proofreading this book, Miryam S. Roddy and
    June Fox

I also want to especially thank and acknowledge my dad, Donald Brody, who was larger than life. Also, I want to thank my mother, Gay Brody, who is ever the lady, and my maternal grandmother Rachel Siegel, whose favorite expression was, "Politeness is to do and say the kindest thing in the kindest way."

CONTENTS

INTRODUCTION

In today's high-tech, fast-paced, increasingly wired world, the importance of human interaction is often overlooked. Perhaps there was a time when you could have been confident that hard work, technical skills, or experience would take you to the top. Unfortunately, this is no longer true. In this highly technological atmosphere, factors other than expertise will be just as crucial to your success.

Happily, one critical factor is something so basic that you started to learn it as a child: good manners. In today's workplace, demonstrating that you are polite, skillful at getting along with others, and proficient at making people feel comfortable and important is more necessary than ever.

Etiquette is an asset in almost every professional situation. The current business environment is far more complex than it once was. For example, women, minorities, and people with disabilities now play vital roles in arenas that were once the exclusive domain of white males. Good manners help you to demonstrate sensitivity and eliminate behaviors that might be considered sexist, racist, or discriminatory.

Good manners also make you more efficient. Once you allow the rules of professional etiquette to guide your behavior, you won't have to spend time soothing ruffled feelings or making up for damaging mistakes.

Professional etiquette is such a powerful tool that it is surprising how often it is neglected. Sometimes we are so busy we feel overwhelmed. We may think there just isn't enough time for niceties like manners. We seriously underestimate their impact, questioning whether they matter, or if anyone really cares.

They do matter. Often it is precisely the little things — a respectful gesture, a subtle courtesy, an unexpected bit of thoughtfulness — that clinch a sale, cement a relationship, or establish a credible professional image. Countless opportuni-

VII

ties are lost as a result of inattention to such "little" things. Graciousness will help you gain new clients and keep you from losing the ones you have. Employees who are treated politely will feel valued and will want to work harder for you. Courtesy can advance your career and enhance your reputation as a consummate professional, while poor manners can place a ceiling on your advancement.

Even if your office environment is quite casual and laid-back, etiquette is necessary and important. Being friendly and polite is a significant advantage in all professional situations.

How are your own "company manners?" You have everything to gain — and nothing to lose — by perfecting them. Here is a list of the 10 most common etiquette errors that people make in the workplace. You can use it to help you to evaluate your own professional etiquette. Be honest with yourself, and see if you recognize any of your own behaviors as you read through the list.

THE 10 MOST COMMON BUSINESS ETIQUETTE ERRORS

1. **Wasting other people's time.** Are you sometimes late for appointments? Do you occasionally arrive unprepared? Have you missed deadlines for turning in assignments? Do you feel that barging into another person's office or interrupting a meeting any time you want is acceptable?

2. **Speaking before thinking.** Listen carefully to yourself. Do you call people by inappropriate nicknames or use forms of address such as "Hon" or "Babe" that could be interpreted as demeaning or insulting? Do you sometimes use humor that is tasteless or crude? Have you ever insulted, criticized, or embarrassed a colleague? Do you gossip or perpetuate rumors?

3. **Dressing unprofessionally, exhibiting sloppy grooming.** Are your clothes too tight, too short, revealing, or unkempt? Do you have ragged nails or messy hair? Look in the mirror: Is this the image you want others to use in assessing you? Is it the image your company wants to project?

4. **Abusing or misusing technology.** Does your beeper or cell phone frequently interrupt conversations or go off in the middle of meetings, even when there is no real emergency? Is it obvious that you use your answering machine to screen unwanted calls? Do you tie up other people's fax machines and waste their paper with many pages of unsolicited materials?

5. **Using poor telephone manners.** Do you ever confuse people by not immediately identifying yourself properly? Do you keep people on "hold" for too long? Do you ever forget to give messages or to return calls promptly? Do you eat during phone conversations or slam down the receiver when you're finished talking?

6. **Greeting people improperly or not at all.** Is your handshake pleasant and reassuring? Or is it as limp as a noodle or painful as a vise? Are you sure you always know when a handshake is appropriate? When visiting another country, do you assume that this is the proper greeting, or do you take the time to learn the proper gestures?

7. **Practicing poor conversational skills.** Do you interrupt when others are speaking? If you ask a question, do you proceed to another topic before the other person can answer? Do your eyes wander when someone else is speaking?

8. **Letting poor body language undermine your words.**
   Your body language speaks louder and more eloquently
   than words. Do you imply a lack of self-confidence or
   interest by slouching? Do you convey closed-mindedness
   and inflexibility by crossing your arms? Boredom by avert-
   ing your eyes?

9. **Invading other people's privacy or abusing shared
   space.** When you are in someone else's office, do you read
   the papers on his or her desk or listen to his or her telephone conversations? After sharing an office or a conference room, do you sometimes forget to clean up after
   yourself? If you use the last sheet of paper in the copy
   machine, do you leave the tray empty so the next person
   must refill it?

10. **Forgetting — or simply not knowing — table man-
    ners.** Do people ever comment on your picky or over-
    zealous eating habits? Does a formal table setting intim-
    idate you? Do you play a clumsy tug of war with the
    check?

Did you recognize yourself in any of these etiquette blun-
ders? If so, don't worry. You can start immediately to devel-
op the business etiquette skills you need to move ahead, both
personally and professionally.

PROFESSIONAL PRESENCE

ONE

**"Bob, you old &#$!!#,
how the !$#&*! are you!?"**

We use three important types of signals to commu-nicate with each other: visual, vocal and verbal. These signals communicate not only what we think and what we want, but also who we are. The resulting image people formulate of us is our professional presence.

Strong impressions are often made within the first five seconds of meeting someone. This doesn't allow a lot of time for interpreting vocal or verbal cues. However, there are some vocal and verbal signals that can ruin your image almost immediately. Mumbling or cursing are two good examples.

In general, speak slowly enough to be understood and enunciate your words clearly. Act enthusiastic, but not to an extent that makes you appear unprofessional. It is good verbal manners to avoid buzzwords, jargon and sarcasm. Be sure your humor is appropriate. Do not be vulgar or coarse.

The visual signals you send can be even more potent than the vocal or verbal ones. Research shows that the overall impression you make is based on the way you use your voice (vocal), the words you choose (verbal) and your appearance/body language (visual). The visual element consists of all the things people first see when they look at you: your attire, grooming, facial expressions, gestures, and even the way you stand and carry yourself.

Obviously, appearance has a lot to do with whether people perceive you favorably. But this doesn't mean you have to look like a movie star to be successful. It means you have to look, dress and act like a professional.

BODY LANGUAGE

One key component of your visual image is your body language. No matter what words you choose, your posture, your body position, gestures, and facial expressions will either support or undermine your message.

- Posture and position. Standing straight makes people feel more alert and look more confident. Slouching can make you look tired, sloppy or apathetic. It can even give the impression that you are trying to hide, or at least be as inconspicuous as possible. You want to look self-assured, not uncertain or apathetic, so don't slouch. Remember that good posture is just as important when you are seated.

- Movement. Try to keep your movements simple and graceful. Hesitant or jerky motions will make you appear nervous or timid.

- Gestures. Use natural gestures to reinforce your verbal messages, but avoid being overly dramatic. Hands on hips, pounding fists, and crossed arms tend to make other people feel uncomfortable. Pointing a finger at someone will make him or her feel uneasy and defensive. Wringing your hands or playing with things in your pocket makes you appear nervous. A nod is reassuring. It says, "Yes, I understand."

- Facial expressions. Even when you don't think so, your mood is clearly written on your face. A smile says, "Welcome." In the United States, eye contact conveys confidence and trustworthiness, while shifty eyes are considered nervous or sly. Frowning and staring can make people feel uneasy. Keep your expression pleasant. It is possible to discuss something difficult or even upsetting without looking angry or threatening.

GROOMING

You may be wearing your most professional-looking designer suit, but you can destroy your entire image if your hair is in disarray, your nails are chipped, there is a food stain on your blouse or tie, or your breath is bad.

Before you dress, check your clothing carefully. Is everything clean and well pressed? Are there any food or perspiration stains? Can you detect any lint or hairs? Are there missing buttons or a broken zipper? Are your shoes scuffed or soiled? Now is the time to rectify any of these problems.

Before going out the door, take a good, hard look at yourself in a full-length mirror in a well-lit room. Men should check for any "five-o'clock shadow." Women should be sure

3

there are no runs in their stockings or lipstick on their teeth.

Even if you have to get up a little earlier in the morning, be sure you give yourself enough time to handle any last-minute grooming emergencies. If you roll right out of bed, into your clothes, and out the door, that is how you are going to look.

Check your appearance periodically throughout the day for that stray piece of lunchtime spinach between your teeth, any unappetizing coffee or ink stains, or any blotchy or caked makeup.

While doing an etiquette program once, one female participant complained about another woman, without mentioning a name, who didn't wash her hands after going to the bathroom. At that point another female participant said, "Are you talking about so and so (and named a name)?" The lesson here? People *do* notice and people *will* talk. So take an extra minute in the bathroom during the workday to wash your hands and freshen up your appearance.

PROFESSIONAL DRESS

You want to enhance your professional image. Select your business wardrobe with an eye toward accomplishing this. What you choose to wear says a great deal about your personality, attitude and professionalism.

A good rule of thumb is to avoid clothing and accessories that are too much of anything. Clothes that are too short, too tight, or too gaudy may call attention to you, but it will not be in a positive way. Avoid anything that is exaggerated or overdone, whether it's clothing, jewelry, a hairstyle or makeup.

Notice what those around you are wearing. Pay particular attention to the clothing choices of people in your organization you consider to be successful. This will give you a good idea of what is accepted and what "works" in your office. You can adapt these general guidelines to suit your own personal style. While the idea is to fit in, it is not necessary to become a carbon copy.

Whatever your current position within your organization, dress for the position you'd like to attain. Appearance has a big impact on how co-workers, clients, customers, and supervisors view you. It is never too early in your career to begin to cultivate your professional image. Aim high. Your appearance also has a strong effect on both how you feel and the way you perform. When you feel confident about your appearance, you feel more competent.

Simple and basic outfits are best. For your business wardrobe, opt for having fewer well-made, classically styled pieces rather than a closet full of trendy pieces of lesser quality. If you choose colors that flatter you and pieces that can be mixed and matched, you will achieve maximum variety at minimum cost.

Every piece in your business wardrobe should meet the following criteria:

- Appropriateness. It should be right for the job, the company, the season, the region, the climate and the setting.

- Size. It must fit correctly. It should flatter you without calling undue attention to your body.

- Message. It should convey good judgment and taste. It should help send the message, "I'm a professional who should be taken seriously."

BUSINESS CASUAL

Until relatively recently, the only time casual dress was acceptable in business was at company-sponsored social affairs: golf tournaments, company picnics, or other kinds of recreational events. Today, many companies allow and even encourage a more relaxed dress code. Some offices have formally sanctioned "Dress Down Days," on either an occasional or a regular basis.

Being able to dress casually and comfortably for work may sound appealing, but it is important not to get too carried away with the idea. "Dress down" does not mean "dress sloppily." There is never a right time in business to display your ripped jeans, short shorts, tank tops, muscle shirts, or T-shirts emblazoned with your favorite political slogans.

Business casual is just that — still business. Therefore, you need to put as much thought into your casual wardrobe as you do into your regular business wardrobe. And there is never an excuse for careless grooming.

Consider the three general principles — appropriateness, size and message — in selecting your business casual wardrobe. Like all business attire, every piece should be flattering, clean and pressed. The accompanying chart provides some specific guidelines.

GUIDELINES FOR BUSINESS CASUAL DRESS

Women
Acceptable attire can include skirts, split skirts (skorts), and well-fitting slacks, worn with blouses or blouse-and-jacket combinations. Flat-heeled shoes with stockings are fine, but sneakers or sandals are only appropriate if you are attending a sporting event.

Men
Acceptable attire can include slacks with button-down shirts, cotton T-shirts with collars, or sweaters. Loafers and slip-on shoes with socks are appropriate, but only wear sneakers or sandals if you're attending a sporting event.

Both
If you feel jeans are appropriate for the setting and occasion, make sure they are completely free of holes or tears. Absolutely no cutoffs!

WARDROBE WISDOM — SYNOPSIS

Here are the essential items to own and suggestions to know for working men and women in order to master proper business professional and casual dress and accessories.

Business Professional (Yes, people still do dress this way!)

<u>Men</u>
• Two-piece wool, wool-blend or cotton blend suit in navy, gray or charcoal (khaki can be OK for a more casual, summer look). At least five two-button, three-button or double-breasted suits in classic styling. European cuts rarely flatter broad-shouldered American men.
• Navy blazer
• Contrasting sport coat and trousers. Plaid is too casual.
• Silk ties (bow ties not recommended) that hit the top or middle of the belt. No over-the-top wild patterns or colors. Burgundy, red and navy work as background colors. Small geometric prints and stripes are good choices. Paisleys with subdued patterns are another option. Tie and suit color should complement each other, but not match.
• Long-sleeve cotton or cotton/polyster blend dress shirts in solid colors. White is best and the safest choice, pale blue is also OK. Light blue and red pinstripes are also acceptable options in some situations. Never wear lavender, peach, plaids, dots, or broad stripes.
• Nylon or thin cotton socks that go over the calf in black, brown or navy.
• Leather lace-up or slip-on shoes. Wingtips are OK for colder climates. Tasseled loafers are less conservative. Black shoes are appropriate with gray, navy or black suits and dark brown shoes are good with tan, brown or beige suits.
• Brown, black or burgundy briefcase, or nice canvas computer bags.

- One ring per hand is OK; no more.
- Good quality watch in sterling silver, gold or stainless steel.

When combining suit, shirt and tie, men should choose one of three options:

1) One solid, two patterns
2) Two solids, one pattern
3) Three patterns (this combination takes skill and practice to coordinate)

Women
- Black, gray or navy suit
- Contrasting jacket and skirt
- Two-piece dress
- Several white, off-white blouses
- Solid color blouses (may be pastels)
- Scarves that pick up colors from the suits
- Neutral or skin-color hosiery
- Black pumps, navy or taupe pumps
- One pair gold, one pair silver earrings
- Black leather handbag
- All-weather coat
- Black, brown or Cordovan briefcase

Business Casual

Men
- Chinos or "Dockers"-type trousers
- Sport shirts with collars or banded necks
- Polo shirts
- Sweater
- Casual loafers or lace-up shoes (with socks)
- Navy blazer

Women

- Casual skirts, slacks or "skorts"
- Neatly pressed chinos or corduroys are acceptable
- Cotton shirts in solids, prints or muted plaids
- Sweaters (not too tight), sweater sets
- Blazers look good over slacks or casual skirt
- Low-heeled shoes or boots — wear stockings or socks

Business Casual Don'ts — Men & Women

- Jeans (of any color), depending on the corporate culture
- Athletic wear (sweat suits, exercise clothes, running suits, etc.)
- T-shirts
- Bare midriffs
- Garments cut low in front or back
- Leggings
- Shorts
- Gym shoes, sneakers or sandals
- Any type of shoes without socks
- Hats, baseball caps, etc.
- Ripped or tattered clothing

GREETINGS AND INTRODUCTIONS

While about to shake hands with a client, he sneezed in his right hand. As I extended my hand anyway knowing it was the proper thing to do, he said, "Why don't we forget shaking? I just sneezed in my hand."

We have all been told that first encounters make a lasting impression. This is quite true, and a favorable first meeting can provide a solid foundation for a positive relationship. Unfortunately, if the first impression is negative, it becomes an obstacle you will have to work hard to overcome.

So what should this businessman above have done as he was about to sneeze? Either use his handkerchief or a tissue, which is held in the left hand.

THE HANDSHAKE

In the United States, the most common and proper business greeting is the handshake. Many people believe that the way a person shakes hands conveys a great deal about his or her personality and competence. A limp handshake is often interpreted as a sign of weakness or lack of confidence. A death grip is often taken as evidence of over-confidence or aggression. It is easy to perfect a professional handshake by remembering three simple steps:

- Say your name and extend your hand. Traditionally, the higher-ranking person initiates the handshake by extending a hand first. However, if that person doesn't do this, go ahead and extend yours. Some men are hesitant about initiating a handshake with a woman, because it used to be considered proper etiquette for a man to wait for a woman to extend her hand first. If there appears to be some hesitation on the part of the man, a woman can simplify matters by extending her hand first.

- Extend your hand at a slight angle, touch thumb joint to thumb joint, and then wrap your fingers firmly — without cutting off the circulation or endangering any bones — around the other person's palm. It's all one smooth movement once you get the hang of it.

- Pump two or three times. Then let go and drop your hand.

TIMING

Knowing how to shake hands in a pleasing way is the first step. But knowing when it is appropriate is just as important. Here are the occasions when it's considered proper etiquette to shake hands:

- During introductions or farewells, whether in one-on-one or group situations

- When greeting someone from outside the company (a client, customer, vendor, or other visitor)

- When you run into a business acquaintance you haven't seen in a while

- When you formalize an agreement

• Whenever your good sense urges you to do so

INTRODUCING YOURSELF

One important and exciting part of business life is meeting new people. Of course, it's always more comfortable when there is someone around to make the introductions. Unfortunately, this is not always the case.

If no one is available to introduce you — or when the person you are with forgets to do it — it is always good manners to introduce yourself. It is also easier than you might think, if you are prepared.

Take a few minutes to prepare a general self-introduction. It should be brief, informative and memorable — a bit like a 10-second commercial. For example: "Hello, I'm Mary Jones. I help people save money on their taxes." Or, "Hello, I'm Mary Jones, I work with people to save them money on their taxes." This type of introduction will almost always encourage the other person to ask, "How do you do that?" or, "Tell me more" — promoting further dialogue. Make your introduction as upbeat and interesting as possible. The results will be well worth the effort.

It's also important to tailor your introduction to the situation. If everyone already knows the name of your company, you don't need to announce it again.

Practice your introduction aloud in front of a mirror until you feel perfectly comfortable with it. Remember to hold your head up, make eye contact, shake hands and smile.

INTRODUCING OTHERS

Have you ever been with a group of people to whom you weren't introduced? If so, you know how uncomfortable that can feel. The unintroduced person usually feels like an outsider — left out, or even invisible. In a meeting, people who don't know everyone present can be distracted from the business at hand while trying to figure out who's who. Some people who find themselves in this situation do not feel confident or assertive enough to introduce themselves to the people they haven't met.

This is an example of an occasion when you can step in and demonstrate your good manners and professional polish. The purpose of making introductions is to not only give names, but to say something about each person so conversation can ensue.

The proper introduction involves three steps:

First mention the name of the person of greatest authority or importance. Gender or age is not the deciding factor. When a client is involved, he or she should be mentioned first.

In our informal business environment, we often use the first names. An introduction should mention first and last names: "Bill Smith, I want you to meet Miryam Roddy."

The second step includes saying something about the person that is being introduced: "Bill Smith, I want you to meet Miryam Roddy, who is Brody Communications Ltd.'s public relations director."

To complete the introduction, go back to the person of highest rank (customer, etc.) and say something about him or her: "Bill Smith, I want you to meet Miryam Roddy, who is Brody Communications Ltd.'s public relations director. Miryam, Bill Smith is the human resource director at XYZ Company — our valued client."

What should you do if you forget the name of someone you need to introduce to another person? The clever way would be to introduce the person you already know. Say, "I don't believe you've met Marjorie Brody, have you?" This will almost always result in the third person saying, "No. We've never met. My name is Frank Black" — or words to that effect.

If no one introduces you to an unfamiliar person, take the initiative. Extend your hand as you say, "My name is Marjorie Brody. I don't believe we've met."

EXCHANGING BUSINESS CARDS

In some countries, the exchange of business cards is governed by time-honored rituals. But in the United States, the circumstances and timing and presenting of cards is not quite as formal.

Either at the beginning or the end of the first encounter is traditionally when business cards are exchanged in this country. If you want to offer your card, ask for the other person's card first. In most cases, the other person will then ask for yours. If not, offer it.

As with the old-fashioned calling card, you can also use your business card to announce your presence by giving it to the receptionist. This is a polite gesture that makes it easier for the receptionist to remember your name and company when informing your host of your arrival.

At meetings, cards are often exchanged prior to the beginning of business to help everyone remember each participant's name and area of expertise. Discreetly referring to a card is far more polite than losing track of the proceedings while you wrack your brain to recall the name of the person sitting at the other end of the table.

Your card can also represent you when you aren't present. You can enclose your card when forwarding materials to someone or when sending a letter to someone with whom you hope to do business in the future.

Before giving your card, ask for the other person's first. Then, give your own business card. It's much more gracious than thrusting your card at them. If the other person doesn't have a business card, but you want their contact information, take your card, cross off the front and get their details on the back (this way you won't accidentally give out their information when distributing your own cards).

There are times and places when handing out business cards is not good etiquette. For example, it is not appropriate to distribute cards during a meal. If you want to initiate a card exchange, wait until everyone is finished eating. If you are at a private dinner party, you may bring your cards with you, but don't give any out unless someone specifically asks you for one.

A good guideline is to be selective in your distribution of business cards. Don't just work your way around the room passing out cards at random. That's not only wasteful, it's obnoxious.

Before giving out your card, think about whether the person might actually need or want to contact you in the future. If the answer is even a possible "yes," then by all means, offer your card. The best way to give your card is to ask for the other person's first. Then you can say, "Let me give you one of mine also." Or, say something like, "If you want to keep in touch, here's my card."

Above all, make sure your business cards suit your professional image. They should be well designed and printed on high-quality paper. They should be free of wrinkles, smudges, and tattered edges.

Keep your cards readily available. Carrying cards in a fixed location in an easily accessible pocket, briefcase, or purse will ensure that they will always be within easy reach.

If your company doesn't give you business cards, consider making them at home on your own computer and printer — there are many software programs that have business card templates. Special perforated paper stock also makes this process easy. Or, you can get a calling card made for yourself, which would have your name, company name, phone number, address and any Internet addresses (e-mail and Web site, if applicable). Having a homemade business card or calling card sure beats ripping a napkin and writing your information on that!

OPENING LINES

It can feel like opening night on Broadway when you have to start a conversation with someone you haven't met before. The curtain has gone up, and the spotlight is on you.

Initiating small talk is an art rather than a science. But it is an important art, because it can help you overcome the awkwardness of first meetings and to connect with people.

Be direct and sincere. Don't try to be cute or funny. Because you don't know the other person yet, your humor might easily be lost or misinterpreted. Here are some polite and proven ways to effectively start a conversation:

- Make an upbeat observation. "This is a very interesting seminar. I've already picked up a lot of valuable information."

- Offer a pleasant self-revelation. "This is my first time in Philadelphia."

- Ask an open-ended question. "How did you manage to get here in all of the snow?"

If your first opening line fails to elicit a response, try another one. The open-ended question should work even if the person is shy. If there is still no response, quietly move on to something or someone else. The last thing you want to do is annoy someone.

TALKING TO ANYONE ABOUT ANYTHING (BUT NOT ANYWHERE)

At times, silence is golden. This is not the case when you're trying to get to know someone. Then, it's just plain awkward.

A little small talk can help you progress from an initial introduction into a comfortable conversation. It can put people at ease and establish a rapport that will help establish a solid relationship.

One of the best things about small talk is that it's an art you can practice just about anywhere, and at anytime. You can be passing a co-worker in the hallway, waiting for an elevator with a supervisor, or arriving at a meeting with a

17

prospective client or customer. It takes only a minute or two to make a connection.

Since you never know when the opportunity to initiate small talk will arise, you should always be prepared with a repertoire of ideas and topics. Some conversational openers that are always appropriate include traffic conditions, sports, or that old standby, the weather. When you're away from your own office, try opening with a favorable comment about the city you are visiting or the event you're attending.

Steer clear of such conversational taboos as religion or income, anything highly controversial, and any intimate details about your life. Avoid the subject of health — whether it is your own or the other person's.

Keeping up with current events will help you add to your repertoire of effective small-talk openers. It is a good idea to read your daily newspaper and a few magazines a month. It is important to read your professional journals, too. When you are in another city for business reasons, read the local paper. Stay alert. Knowing what's going on around you can help you to join in a conversation. Always be careful to keep your comments neutral and positive, especially on subjects that can become inflammatory, and particularly when you are a guest in someone else's city or country.

Listen attentively when others speak. Besides being the polite thing to do, this will help you learn a great deal about the other person. You will pick up valuable clues about the best way to guide the conversation.

What not to do when greeting or introducing someone

I once witnessed the following exchange: A manager introduced one of his employees to a client with whom he was meeting. The employee's name was unusual. After introducing the employee with the unusual name, the manager said, "Can you believe that any mother would name a child that?"

It's important to remember that more and more business

professionals are multicultural — many ethnic groups comprise today's workplace. What is an unusual name for you may be perfectly normal elsewhere — and it's poor etiquette to mention any observed differences, anyway.

I've also heard others comment on various peoples' names by saying, "Wow that's a tough name." Once a woman introduced herself to me as "Polly." She had moved to the United States from China within the last six months. After establishing a rapport with her, I said, "What's your real name, I can't believe it's Polly?" She said, "I got tired of Americans making fun of my name, so I changed mine to Polly."

Choose your opportunities to have conversations carefully. Avoid discussing any private or confidential information in elevators, restrooms, hallways, public transportation, restaurants, or even office cubicles.

NETWORKING

Yet another old adage with a golden nugget of truth is: "Your success often depends as much on who you know as what you know."

It would be impossible to overstate the importance of establishing and maintaining an extensive network of contacts. Many people are intimidated by the prospect of having to network. But the contacts you make today can open doors for you throughout your career.

OPPORTUNITIES TO NETWORK

If you feel nervous about the idea of networking, consider this: You have already been doing it all your life, without stopping to think about it. Everyone you have ever met is part of a network you have already constructed, and it is larger than you think. It is made up of all your friends, neighbors, social club or sports team members, your doctors, dentist, banker, your accountant and religious leader, as well as any current and former co-workers, customers and competitors. A surprising number of people are part of your personal network.

There are opportunities to network all around you — even in places you would least expect. You have already found many opportunities to add to your network. Now

21

that you are aware of this, you simply have to train yourself to channel your efforts into furthering your professional goals.

Always keep your eyes open for networking occasions.

Here are some opportunities for networking within an organization:

- **Sports teams.** If your company has any, join in. It doesn't matter at all if you aren't a pro. Learn as much as you can about the activity, arrive equipped, and have fun!

- **Lunch.** This is a great time to get to know your colleagues on a more relaxed, informal basis. Don't eat alone at your desk; if you do, you are relinquishing a good opportunity to network. Besides, everybody needs an occasional break from the office.

- **Look beyond your own position or department.** Volunteer to assist with company-wide events or activities. This is a great way to demonstrate your versatility and your team spirit.

There's a big world out there. Get out and circulate!

Here are some networking opportunities outside the office:

- **Volunteer.** Become involved with a charitable organization or cause in your community. Donate your time, not just money. The good feeling you will get from helping others will be an extra bonus.

- **Join organizations and participate actively.** Naturally, it is important to join professional or trade organizations related to your career. But there are many other good opportunities as well, such as participating in programs given by your local Chamber of Commerce, or running for a place on the school board. There are social groups and groups that form around a specific interest, such as investment groups, book clubs and photography clubs. Speak up at meetings, serve on committees and attend the events.

SOME DO'S AND DON'TS OF NETWORKING

Networking is a powerful and natural tool for making new contacts and forming new personal and professional relationships. However, there are certain protocols that should govern networking situations.

WORKING A ROOM

"Working a room" doesn't mean flitting from person to person, pumping hands, and aggressively handing out your business card. It doesn't mean scanning the room for bigger and better opportunities when you are already in the middle of a conversation.

It simply means being alert for networking opportunities. It means keeping your eyes — and your mind — open.

When you are attending a party or event where you know the host or someone else, take advantage of any offers they extend to introduce you to people. If you don't receive any offers, or if there is a particular person or group of people you would like to meet, it is perfectly appropriate to ask for an introduction or introduce yourself.

What if you walk into a party or event and find that you don't know another soul in the room? First, don't panic. Next, you have three options:

Option number one:

• Find the farthest out-of-the-way corner and hide there for the duration of the event. This practically guarantees you a miserable time.

Option number two:

- Stand there and hope someone comes up to you. Of course, if you choose this option, chances are you will find yourself standing alone and feeling awkward for quite a while.

Option number three:

- Find someone else who is alone, approach that person with a friendly smile, and introduce yourself.

If you choose option number three, congratulations are in order. It means you recognized and decided to make use of a prime networking opportunity.

If the idea of approaching a total stranger makes you uncomfortable, bear this in mind: You are probably doing that person a tremendous favor by initiating a conversation. He or she will probably feel grateful to you. There are very few people who actually enjoy standing alone in a crowded room.

In a large group, approach a person that is alone or a gathering of three or more people. Two people might be engrossed in a real conversation and wouldn't want to be disrupted.

As discussed in Chapter Two, initiating a conversation can be relatively simple and painless if you prepare ahead. Have your professional handshake and 10-second self-introduction ready. Look the person in the eye. Ask a question or use one of the other suggestions for opening lines offered earlier: an upbeat observation, a pleasant self-revelation or an open-ended question.

If the two of you get along well, be sure you exchange business cards before parting company. Later, when you return to your home or office, note right on the card where you met the person and any pertinent information you recall about him or her before filing it away. If you collect a lot of cards at an event, put them together and photocopy them on one or two pages. Indicate the date and event. Of course, having a manual "Rolodex" or an electronic database is the best way to be organized with the cards you collect.

You shouldn't worry if your networking attempts don't meet with success every time. Sometimes, despite our best efforts, we are going to run into people we genuinely dislike or don't wish to see again. When this happens, the best thing to do is to cut the conversation short in a polite but firm way. "It was nice meeting you, but I must be going now" is a perfectly adequate way to bow out. But no matter how you feel about the person, don't forget to smile and say goodbye.

RECIPROCATING

Reciprocation is the Golden Rule of networking etiquette. So far, we have been focusing on how networking will help you. But this can't be totally one-sided. Networking works best when it is working both ways. You will depend on the people in your network for support and assistance, and you want them to look to you for the same kind of support. You don't want to always be the one seeking a favor. Providing a favor will make it easier for you if you need to ask for one later.

MAKING THE CONTACT

We have described a number of ways to initiate networking contacts. For example, you can expand your network simply by taking advantage of opportunities to introduce yourself to new people at parties or events.

You can also initiate contact by writing a letter, placing a phone call, or sending an e-mail. Which method you choose will largely depend on what feels most comfortable to you. It will also depend on the particular circumstances, your connection to someone who is willing to provide an introduction, and your relationship to the person you are actually contacting. (If you're following up on a referral, be sure to mention the name of your mutual acquaintance at the beginning of your note or call.)

Clearly identify your personal objectives before you initiate contact. Are you hoping for a promotion? A new job? A new customer or client? Then decide precisely what you would like this new contact to know about you. Make a list of the points you want to cover.

At the same time, don't get so caught up in presenting yourself and achieving your specific objectives that you forget to be a good listener. Be sure to convey a genuine interest in what the other person has to say. Even if he or she can't help you get a particular job or promotion right now, this contact could become a mentor for you, possibly providing invaluable advice and guidance throughout your career. If you make a positive impression, there is always the possibility that this new contact may be able to help you in the future or that you might be able to help them.

During your initial conversation, see if you can learn something about the other person's needs and goals. Listen for clues that can help you discover how you might assist this new contact. If you can offer him or her some kind of help, it will be much easier for you to ask for assistance somewhere down the line.

FOLLOWING UP

Follow up the initial contact with a brief note. Be sure to express your appreciation if the person provided you with any information or other assistance. If not, just let the person know you are grateful for the time he or she spent talking to you.

Once you have established a connection, find ways to keep it alive. For example, if you see a magazine or newspaper article that might interest the person, it would be a thoughtful gesture to forward it along with a brief note. Acknowledge any awards, promotions, or positive publicity your contact receives with a congratulatory note. Call to say hello or to meet for lunch.

Remember, it is people who constitute a network. Business cards sitting in a Rolodex or names in a database can't do anything to help you. They are just pieces of paper, unless you put in the time and effort to keep the personal connection going. If you do, the results will be more than worth it. Too often people wait until they need help before making connections. Do it when you need nothing; be willing to help others — they will definitely be there for you.

THE JOB INTERVIEW

There is probably no bigger test of the ability to function professionally and gracefully under pressure than the job interview.

Interviewers come in all shapes and sizes. Some interviewers go out of their way to make candidates feel as comfortable as possible. Others choose to apply extra pressure to determine whether the prospective employee has courage and poise under fire. As Forrest Gump observed about life and boxes of chocolates, "You never know what you're going to get." It is walking into the unknown that makes the prospect of an interview so alarming for many people.

But while each interview is different, you won't go wrong if you follow a few general guidelines.

BEFORE THE INTERVIEW

Although it is during the interview that you make your impression, you can do a lot beforehand to help ensure that the impression will be favorable.

Here are some areas that you should keep in mind as you prepare for that all-important meeting:
- Do your homework. Find out everything you can about the company. Visit the firm's Web site. Request brochures

29

and an annual report, if available. Search the Internet and library for articles and information about the company. If possible, go to the site the day before and wait for lunch time. When employees start walking outside, note what they're wearing, the general atmosphere and their attitudes.

- Think about your appearance. Select clothing that reflects your professionalism. Pay close attention to your grooming. (See Chapter One for more details on how to dress to make the best impression.)

- Practice. Some interviewers simply start by asking, "Tell me about yourself." Prepare and rehearse a brief verbal resume. Give special attention to any work experience and skills that relate to the specific position for which you are interviewing. If possible, get a friend to role-play with you. A friend who acts as "the interviewer" may surprise you with questions you didn't anticipate, which can be a great help to you in preparing.

- Revise your resume and type a list of references. Be ready to answer any and all questions about your resume. For example, "Did sales increase while you were at Mid-Atlantic?" or "Why did you leave your job at the magazine?" Have a list of references with accurately updated telephone numbers ready to offer. Ask each person on your list for permission to use him or her as a reference before submitting the list.

DURING THE INTERVIEW

You want to be sure your image says "professional" from the moment you walk in the door.

Here are some actions that are not only appropriate during an interview, but are entirely necessary for creating a positive impression:

- **Be on time.** If possible, allow yourself an extra 10 minutes in case you have problems with parking, finding the elevator, or locating the right office. Use any leftover time to check your appearance one last time.

- **Shake hands.** If the interviewer doesn't offer his or her hand, you should offer yours. Make sure your handshake is firm and confident. (For more on the art of handshaking, see Chapter Two.) Remember to smile and make eye contact.

- **Wait to be seated.** If the interviewer doesn't offer you a seat, ask where you should sit.

- **Display quiet confidence.** Sit up straight and tall in your chair, and look the interviewer directly in the eye. Don't fidget or squirm. Don't chew gum or smoke. Speak clearly. Keep your hands out of your pockets and away from your mouth.

- **Emphasize your strengths.** Tell the interviewer exactly why you are the best candidate for the position. Show him or her that you know something about the company.

- **Keep your answers brief and to the point.** Nervousness sometimes causes people to become chatty. Don't ramble or stray off on unrelated tangents. Answer the interviewer's questions in a manner that is honest, straightforward and succinct.

- **Don't use jargon or slang.** You want to sound articulate, knowledgeable and professional. Never try to be funny during an interview.

- **Keep your cool.** No matter what the interviewer asks you, don't allow yourself to become annoyed or antagonized. If a question seems so inappropriate that you truly don't wish to answer, you can ask the interviewer calmly and politely how the answer to that question pertains to the position. If the interviewer persists and you are still uncomfortable, you can hold your ground by stating that you would be happy to discuss any information that would truly help determine your qualifications and interest in the position.

- **Ask for the job.** Acting coy or playing hard to get are unattractive and ineffective strategies. Let the interviewer know you would like the position and state your reasons why.

- **Establish the "next step."** Ask the interviewer when he or she expects a decision to be made and when you might expect to be contacted. If the interviewer needs more information from you, establish a definite time when you will provide it.

- **End on a positive note.** Even if you decide you don't want the position after all, smile, shake hands, and pleasantly thank the interviewer for seeing you.

AFTER THE INTERVIEW

After the interview, proper etiquette demands that you send a note of thanks for being extended the interview opportunity. In addition, it is perfectly acceptable to follow up with a phone call, within certain guidelines.

Send the thank-you note immediately. In addition to thanking the interviewer for his or her time, reemphasize your interest in the position, and restate some of the main reasons why you are the best candidate for the job. If you have decided that you are not interested, you should still send a thank-you note for the time and attention that were given to you. It's the polite thing to do, and someday another, more appealing, position may open up at the same company. The interviewer might change jobs or companies at some point, and you may be interested in speaking with him or her again about a different position.

If the interviewer has told you that a decision about the position will probably be made within a week, check in at the end of the week. If you learn that you didn't get the position, try to get some feedback from the interviewer. It may not be what you'd like to hear, but it could be of great value to you in preparing for future interviews. Of course, don't make a nuisance of yourself by phoning every day.

Whatever happens, an interview is good experience. If it didn't go the way you hoped, review it mentally to see how you might have presented yourself more effectively. The next interview will be better.

If you don't get the job, get feedback why so you can improve the next time.

BUSINESS DINING

Several consultants were taking out their clients to lunch. A junior consultant got an itch on his back while cutting his food. He took his fork, scratched his back, and then continued to eat with it.

D ining together gives people an opportunity to get to know each other outside the confines of the office. But don't be misled by the change in atmosphere. Whether you are the host or a guest, business is still the first item on the menu. And you still need to know the correct etiquette guidelines for the business meal.

Most people know that you should never put your elbows on the table or reach across someone else's plate to grab the salt. But for conducting business, it is real "mind-your-manners" restaurant dining that is in order. Are your manners sufficiently polished to smoothly handle the challenge of the business lunch or dinner?

My experience shows that there are many opportunities to learn and hone one's etiquette skills as they relate to business meals.

For example, I was told a story about three business associates who went out for lunch. One associate was cutting his meat with a serrated edge knife, and he wanted to butter his bread. Before buttering the bread, he licked his knife and then stuck it in the butter. Now I doubt very much he made a good impression on his colleagues. Can you imagine the outcome of the meal if his dinning companions were clients or prospects?

BREAKFAST, LUNCH, OR DINNER?

Business can be conducted during any meal. But these days, when people wish to conduct business over a meal, lunch is frequently the meal of choice. Lunch is often the most practical and comfortable option, because it takes place during regular business hours. A lunchtime meeting will cause fewer conflicts with obligations outside of work.

Dinners are generally expected to be more social in nature, even when there is business to be conducted. A dinner invitation may include spouses or significant others. When it does, it is only polite to keep the conversation more general so that the other people present won't feel extraneous and awkward.

And, if you are at a formal dinner and notice someone making an etiquette gaffe, the best course of action would be to carry on as if nothing happened. You certainly don't want to make a scene.

Business breakfasts have become increasingly popular because they generally take less time than other meals. If a brief meeting is all that is needed, a business breakfast will do quite nicely. Some organizations routinely schedule breakfasts before official business hours so that no time is lost from the workday.

HOSTING A BUSINESS LUNCH

If you do the inviting, then you are the host. This means that you make the plans and you pay the bill. Hosting a business meal professionally and productively requires some thinking and planning. Do not confuse the business lunch with your usual, run-of-the-mill midday repast. Cafeteria vending machine or fast-food fare is not appropriate.

As with any business or social event, there are some essential factors to consider, such as location, food and comfort. Before planning a business lunch, first determine your specific reasons for wanting to host it. Is it a substitute for an in-office meeting, or is it simply providing a pleasant way for you to cultivate your network? Is your objective to court a prospective client or to enhance your relationship with a current client? Are you exploring an employment prospect? Is it to reward an individual or your staff for a job well done? Is it being used to celebrate a holiday or individual milestone such as a retirement or an employment anniversary?

Many organizations have specific guidelines as to appropriate reasons and occasions for business meals, their frequency, and the proper protocol to follow. Sometimes the guidelines are written, but often they are simply passed along via word-of-mouth. For example, it was one insurance company's procedure to entertain clients only after they had purchased insurance. When an insurance representative who was unfamiliar with the policy took some prospective clients to lunch before they had formalized their purchase, he was reprimanded. Before making plans, find out if your company has any guidelines that should be followed.

SELECTING A RESTAURANT

Having established that a business lunch is appropriate, your next decision is the setting. It's a good idea to set up a file of restaurants that have an atmosphere, clientele, and service that is business-friendly. Try any new restaurants or restaurants you haven't visited for six or more months before bringing your guests there.

At times you may find yourself hosting a lunch in a town other than your own. If possible, do some advance research. The Internet can be a great resource for finding good restaurants in a particular city. If there is no time for research before you arrive, you may be able to ask ·the concierge at your hotel to suggest some suitable restaurants. Of course, it is always appropriate and considerate to ask your guest if he or she has any favorite places.

Always consider your guest in making your choice. The location should be convenient for him or her. Try to find out if there are any specific dietary requirements or food preferences. If you are uncertain about these, be sure to pick a restaurant that offers a wide range of selections.

INVITING YOUR GUESTS

Call your guest at least one week and, if possible, two weeks in advance to schedule a date and time for lunch. Be ready to offer a few alternative dates and times. Politely inquire whether he or she has any particular preferences regarding food or the choice of a restaurant. Be open and flexible.

Let your guest know if you plan to invite any other people to join you at lunch, so he or she can be prepared. It is also a good idea to mention if there is a specific topic you want to discuss, so he or she can be ready. People appreciate having time to gather together any information or pertinent materials.

MAKING RESERVATIONS

A couple of minutes spent telephoning a restaurant for a reservation can save untold time and embarrassment on the day of your business lunch. No matter how charming a host you are or how congenial the guest, no one likes to waste precious time waiting for a table to become available in a busy restaurant.

In addition to the time and date of the lunch, tell the restaurant how many people you expect to have in your party. If anyone in your party has a physical disability requiring special accommodations, mention that as well. You may also wish to specify whether you want your table to be located in a smoking or non-smoking section. If the number of guests change, inform the restaurant in advance. If you must cancel, cancel the reservations.

GREETING YOUR GUESTS

Confirm the day and time with your guest the day before or the morning of the appointment. Give your guest directions to the restaurant as well as the phone number. Most people appreciate it when you offer parking information as well.

If you haven't met your guest face to face before, offer a description of yourself. To make it as easy as possible for him or her to identify you, mention the color of the coat or clothing you expect to wear as well as your height and hair color.

Arrive early. Immediately check in at the reservation desk to confirm your reservation. Then, wait in the lobby for your guest to arrive.

If there are a number of people in your party, try to wait until everyone has arrived before you ask to be seated. However, it isn't polite to keep everyone waiting for one or two guests who are more than 10 minutes late. If this happens, escort the other members of your party to the table, arrange for them to be seated and order drinks. Then inform the reservation desk of your location so your late-arriving guests can join you. If the guest is 15 minutes late, it is appropriate to call him or her. If it is just the two of you, you should wait at least one half hour before sitting down or leaving the restaurant. If you leave, give a note to the restaurant host to be given to your guest should he or she arrive. It's also a nice gesture to leave a tip for the server.

ORDERING

"Good afternoon, my name is Chris. I'll be your server today." In reality, Chris is much more. Your server is someone who can be very helpful in making your business lunch a success. Take a good look at Chris, so you can easily and quickly recognize him or her later if you have a problem or request.

If your server doesn't offer his or her name, don't snap your fingers, stand up and wave frantically, or shout out "honey," "sweetie," or "garçon" to attract his or her attention. With a little patience, you can usually request service by catching your server's eye or with a discreet wave of the fingers. If all else fails, say "waiter," "waitress," or "server" in a calm and gentle voice.

ORDERING DRINKS

Before taking your lunch order, your server will probably ask if you and your guest would like a drink. The best way to handle this is to defer to your guest. If your guest orders a drink, you may, too. If your guest doesn't want one, don't order one for yourself. The once popular three-martini lunch has disappeared. Drinking is not a mandatory part of the business meal and, in fact, may have a negative impact on your ability to think and function in your most professional manner. If your guest orders a cocktail, you must order something, but it doesn't have to be alcohol. You could say, "I am not having a cocktail, but feel free to have one." Above all, you don't want your guest to feel uncomfortable. If your guest orders a second drink, it's time to tell your server that you want to order."

If your guest indicates a preference for wine, don't be intimidated. White wine generally goes with fish or fowl and red goes with meat. However this is only a guideline, not an unbreakable rule. As with everything, wine is a matter of personal taste.

It is never polite to push wine or any other alcoholic beverage on a guest who doesn't want it. And it is always appropriate for you to order a non-alcoholic beverage for yourself if you prefer not to drink. However, if wine is being served as part of the meal and you would rather not have any, don't turn your wineglass upside down. Simply say, "No, thank you."

ORDERING FOOD

Give your guest sufficient "quiet time" to review the menu, even if you know it by heart. You might briefly make some suggestions about some of the restaurant's specialties. As a guest, select mid- to upper mid-price range. If the host recommends a more expensive item, feel free to order it. As host, you should order in a similar price range to your guest.

Allow your guest to order first and follow his or her lead. For instance, if your guest orders soup or a salad, you should also.

When it comes to ordering, the less fuss you make the better. Don't grill your server about what is in each dish or how it is prepared. Of course, if you have certain allergies or dietary restrictions, you may make inquiries and requests to accommodate them. But do so as simply and as matter-of-factly as possible.

Avoid foods that you know will be messy or difficult to eat. Even if the restaurant serves the best spaghetti or French onion soup in the world, wait for a non-business visit to order it.

PAYING THE CHECK

It's been said earlier, but is worth repeating: If you are the host, you are responsible for paying the check. Whether you are a man or a woman, this is proper etiquette.

What isn't proper etiquette is playing tug-of-war with the bill. If a male guest feels uncomfortable about his female host paying the bill, a polite, non-argumentative approach is for her to say, "The Magic Mirror Corporation would like you to be our guest."

The host can avoid this problem altogether by making payment arrangements in advance of the lunch. That way, the bill will not be presented in front of the guest.

You may quietly review the bill, but don't pull out your calculator to check the addition. If you do find an error, don't cause a commotion at the table. Calmly excuse yourself and take the bill to the server's station to resolve the problem.

If possible, pay by credit card. It's the quickest and most discreet means of settling the bill. If you do pay cash, you may ask for a receipt for business purposes.

LEAVING A TIP

Don't make a production out of calculating the tip. But be sure to check the bill to see if it has already been included (especially if you are dining with a large party).

The tip is typically 15 to 20 percent of the total bill. This can be easily calculated by figuring 10 percent, and then adding half that amount (for 15 percent) or doubling the amount (for 20 percent). In addition, if there was a wine steward (sommelier) who helped you order wine, an additional tip is required.

If the service is bad, you're not obligated to leave a tip (or a standard 15 percent to 20 percent), but tell the server and/or the manager why.

ADDITIONAL TIPPING

The tip for the server and the wine steward (if any) may all be included in your credit card total. Or you may choose to leave the server's tip in cash on the table. Other service personnel (such as coatroom and garage attendants) should be paid directly. It is also polite to say "thank you" for all services rendered.

Here are some guidelines for tipping other restaurant personnel:

Sommelier	Coatroom Attendant	Garage Attendant
$3 to $5 per bottle or 15 percent	$1 per coat	$1 to $2

TABLE MANNERS

Good table manners are a must at any business dining occasion, whether you are a guest or the host. Table manners weren't invented to make dining more difficult. Quite the contrary: They make the whole experience more pleasant by ensuring that no one's behavior offends anyone.

Most of what you need to know about proper behavior at the table is just common sense.

Keep these guidelines in mind:

- **Be polite.** Don't put your handbag or briefcase on the table; put it on your lap or on the floor. Wait until after the meal is ordered before starting to discuss business. When food is being passed to you, say "please" and "thank you." Wait until everyone has been served before eating (unless the host insists that you begin before the food gets cold). This is common where there are more than four people at the table.

- **Be neat.** Always chew with your mouth closed. Wait until you've swallowed your food before speaking. Don't gesture with a utensil in your hand, especially if it has food on it. When eating bread or rolls, don't butter the entire piece of bread or roll at once. Break the bread or roll in half, then tear a piece at a time and butter it as you are ready to eat it. Avoid ordering messy foods. If you drop a utensil, don't pick it up. Politely ask the server for a replacement.

- **Be pleasant.** Don't complain about the food or criticize the service. The host can leave the table and deal with bad service. Guests should say nothing.

- **Be considerate.** It's important to check your grooming throughout the day, but please not at the dining table. If you want to comb your hair or reapply some lipstick before leaving the restaurant, by all means do so, but only in the restroom — never at the table. The same is true for using toothpicks or blowing your nose.

- **Be thoughtful about smoking.** If you're a smoker, don't assume that your guest or your host won't mind sitting in the "smoking section." You need to politely ask. Some people have allergies or simply find cigarette smoke offensive while they are eating. As a considerate host, you should refrain from smoking unless your guest smokes. As a polite guest, you should ask your host's permission before lighting up. It is never appropriate to smoke during a meal. Wait until everyone has finished eating. Best bet — don't do it.

You can truly demonstrate your social manners, and save the day, by making your guest feel welcome at the table — even if he or she makes an etiquette gaffe.

A young engineer I know often describes herself as coming from a family who is more interested in survival than etiquette. She became engaged to a physician. His family, for generations, paid close attention to all etiquette details. When this engineer met his family for the first time, she had dinner at their home. She was ushered into a formal dining room with crystal chandeliers, linen table cloth, sterling silver place settings, antique china and crystal glasses. She was seated to the right of the host, her future father-in-law. Servers brought in the food. She picked up what she thought was a roll, and instead of breaking it in half, she took a bite of it. As her teeth sunk in, she realized she had just bitten into a baked potato! Rather than embarrassing their future daughter-in-law, the mother-in-law and future sisters-in-law picked up their baked potatoes and took bites as well. Now that's classy!

USING DISHES AND UTENSILS CORRECTLY

Given the popularity of fast food and ultra-casual dining establishments, it's not surprising that so many people are baffled by place settings with multiple plates, knives, forks, and spoons. Most people probably wish they had a map to tell them which glasses are theirs and which are their neighbor's. No need to panic!

Table Setting

Just keep the following guidelines in mind:

• Your food dishes (like the bread and butter plate) are always on your left. It is easy to remember this by noticing that both "food" and "left" have four letters.

By knowing this, you will avoid situations like I recently encountered. At a roundtable conference dinner I attended once, the person sitting next to me on the left obviously didn't know which was his food. He proceeded to take my roll. I decided I could always get another one or didn't need a roll at all — rather than cause a disruption or embarrass this man. His friend sitting across the table, however, yelled across the table: "Tony you just took the lady's roll and screwed up all of our bread plates." This poor man wanted to slide under the table.

- Your beverage containers (including coffee cup and saucer) are on your right. Remember that both "drink" and "right" have five letters.

But what about those utensils — that daunting array of salad, entree, and dessert forks and soup, coffee, and dessert spoons? How can you tell which is which and, just as important, which is yours?

There are several variations on the basic place setting. The most correct is the outside-in place setting. With this setting, forks are on the left and knives and spoons are on the right. Diners are expected to work their way through the utensils, from both sides, from the outside to the inside.

To be ready to face any variation gracefully and correctly, you need to learn to identify utensils by their shape and size. That way, you'll recognize them wherever they are! For instance, the soupspoon has a bigger bowl than the teaspoon and the salad fork is smaller than the entree fork. As always, when in doubt, observe your host or others around you.

If you find that you have used your entree fork to eat your salad, there is no need to make an issue of it. Often you can quietly substitute another utensil in your place setting for the one you've used. Or, without drawing undue attention to yourself, quietly ask for a replacement.

UTENSILS -- Rest Position

UTENSILS -- Finished Position

SOCIALIZING WITH COLLEAGUES

W henever you meet with a supervisor, client, or hot prospect in an elegant restaurant or a conference room you know you have to be on your best professional behavior. But what if the setting is the company picnic or office party? What is appropriate at a sport stadium, a concert, or some other "unofficial" locale?

No matter how casual the setting or how festive the occasion, business relationships are still business. A day at the ballpark is a great way for you and your supervisor, client, or colleague to get to know one another outside the formal confines of the office. Just remember: Your behavior at today's ballgame is the behavior your companion will recall at tomorrow's board meeting. Dress appropriately and be yourself, but yourself at your very best. Above all, smile and enjoy yourself. You can easily make a positive impression and still have a good time.

IF YOU ARE THE HOST

Whatever the event or circumstances, your first duty as a host is always the same: to make sure that your guest has a good time. Often this requires a little pre-event planning on your part in terms of providing transportation and arranging for tickets or other types of seating.

If you are taking your guest to the opera or a hockey game and have never attended one before, learn everything you can about opera or hockey before you go. Understanding what you are seeing will allow you to discuss it intelligently with your guest, as well as enhancing your enjoyment of the event. Make sure that your reactions to what is taking place on the field or onstage are appropriate. Refrain from booing, hissing, or "coaching" from the stands, even if your favorite team is losing and it's the playoffs. At a concert, play, or ballet applaud only when appropriate.

If you will be expected to participate rather than watch — in a game of golf, for example — be sure you know the rules and have the equipment you will need. Before the day arrives, brush up on your skills.

Make sure your guest is comfortable as soon as you arrive. If appropriate, provide food and drinks. If the event is a party, make sure that all necessary introductions are made.

Finally, take the opportunity to be a good listener. Whenever possible, invite your guest to talk about himself or herself. You may gain valuable insight into his or her interests, family, and personality.

THE OFFICE PARTY

There are two ways you don't want to be remembered after an office party. First, you don't want to be remembered for becoming the center of attention by dancing with a lampshade on your head. Avoid being remembered for your "colorful" behavior by following this simple advice: Don't get drunk. Even if you think you can "hold your liquor," limit your consumption. While under the influence, you may not have complete control over everything you say or do. However, you will still be held accountable.

You also don't want to be remembered as the person who snubbed your colleagues by not showing up. Make sure you are there. Attendance at the company office party is not optional. Whether you think so or not, your absence will be noticed and noted.

Arrive on time. Making a late entrance won't make people think you are important. It will just make them think you are rude.

Now that we have you there, here are some ways to help make your presence a hit:

Be cordial. Smile and be friendly to everyone. Take advantage of this opportunity to expand your network, by initiating conversations with people outside your existing circle of co-workers and friends. Try to keep business talk to a minimum.

Don't initiate or participate in office gossip. And don't make yourself the subject of tomorrow's office gossip by flirting. Off-color jokes or offensive stories are inappropriate under any circumstances.

Be sure to say hello to the boss. Use your most engaging small-talk techniques. Be pleasant, but respectful. If you don't usually call your boss by his or her first name, don't start now.

Don't leave too soon. Even if the party is dull and you're dying to escape 10 minutes after you arrive, stay for an appropriate length of time. Be attentive to your body language. It's very bad manners to let people see how bored you are.

Thank your hosts. After the party, send a thank-you note to the organizers.

OTHER SOCIAL FUNCTIONS

You can apply all the guidelines described in the "Office Party" section to any social encounter with your colleagues. As with the office party, your attendance is expected. This doesn't mean that every Friday night you have to leave your spouse and children alone to go drinking with your colleagues. It only means that you should make a point of joining in the outside-of-work activities once in a while, even if it's only to accompany your co-workers when they go out to lunch.

Be discreet. Refrain from making any major personal revelations. An evening out with the office gang is not a time to play true confessions. If others share details of their private lives with you, refrain from judging or criticizing them. For instance, if a co-worker describes a quarrel he or she had with a spouse, don't offer your opinion or advice. Just listen attentively and sympathetically.

This brings the subject back to alcohol. Drinking too much can make you drop your guard and loosen your tongue. Don't feel that you have to keep having drinks to show that you're one of the gang. You can be sociable and still remain sober. As soon as you have reached your limit, switch to something non-alcoholic.

If an outing will include your family or a companion, brief them ahead of time about what is appropriate in terms of dress, topics of conversation, and, if you think it is necessary, general behavior. Remember that their actions and words will reflect on you.

**"Your meat looks good.
Can I have a bite?"**

THE TELEPHONE

Opportunity rarely knocks anymore. These days, it usually calls first. Every single call that comes in to you and your company has to be handled with consummate professionalism competence and courtesy.

WHEN THE TELEPHONE RINGS

Good telephone etiquette begins before you even say hello. You should answer all calls within three rings.

No matter what you are doing or how hassled you feel, when you answer the telephone your voice and manners should immediately communicate your professionalism and your readiness to be of service. Take a deep breath before you pick up the phone. Then smile. This may sound silly, but the smile on your face comes through in your voice.

Immediately identify yourself, using your full name. Include a verb so you don't sound abrupt. For example, "Victoria Smith speaking" or "This is Victoria Smith" is better than just "Victoria Smith." If you share a phone with other colleagues, be sure to include the department name. For example, "Marketing, Victoria Smith speaking."

If the call is coming in from the outside, include your company name. For example, "Telfair Manufacturing, Victoria Smith speaking. How may I help you?"

SCREENING YOUR CALLS

At times you may be too busy to take calls. There is nothing wrong with asking your assistant to screen your calls as long as you aren't "in" for some people and "out" for others. If you don't wish to be disturbed, the assistant should say: "Mr. Shawn isn't available right now. Is there anything I can help you with?"

"Okay, he's just decided that he's not in."

Whether you are available or not, callers should never be put through the third degree before they're allowed to speak with you. Make sure your assistant does not demand to know who is calling before saying whether you are available, which would give the definite impression that you are available to certain people, but not to others.

If you use voice mail to answer your calls, your outgoing message should include the time you expect to return or to be available. Change it on a regular basis. Make sure that anyone who might answer your phone when you are away from your desk has accurate information about your anticipated time of return.

CALLING BACK

The rule is simple when it comes to returning telephone calls: the sooner the better, and always within 24 hours. If you can't return the call yourself within a reasonable period of time, have someone else return it for you. Even if you can't help the caller, the polite procedure is to call back and let him or her know so he or she can start looking elsewhere to address her needs.

SCHEDULING A CONVERSATION

When you tell someone that you will call at a specific time, you have scheduled an appointment. The same is true if you arrange for someone to call you at a specific time. Just as you would not simply ignore an appointment you made to meet someone somewhere, you should never "stand up" someone who is waiting to speak with you.

If you find that you won't be available at the pre-arranged time, let the person know right away or, at the very least, have someone else call to let him or her know. Apologize for the inconvenience you have caused and reschedule the appointment. Be sure to thank the person for his or her understanding.

HOLDING A CONVERSATION

When you are on the phone, your full attention should be on the person with whom you are speaking. This is true no matter what else is going on around you. This means no side conversations with co-workers. If you are talking to someone in your office and the phone begins to ring, complete your conversation before you pick up the receiver.

Avoid distractions. Try to keep background noises to a minimum. Turn off the radio. Close the windows or the door. If people around you are making noise, try to move to another area, or ask them to be quiet.

Concentrate on listening. That means no doodling, typing, straightening papers, cleaning out your desk, or planning your lunch order — unless it is related to the call. Be responsive to the caller's statements and questions. A well placed "I see" or "Uh-huh" now and then reassures the speaker that you're still awake and interested. Of course, if you are using headphones in order to get the caller computer information, that is OK.

Put callers on hold only when it's absolutely necessary. Ask for permission first and wait for a response. If you interrupt to answer another call, keep the first caller on hold just long enough to take a message. The first caller always takes priority.

If you absolutely must put a caller on hold, don't let him or her languish there for long periods of time. People feel abandoned and trapped in limbo when left on hold for too long. Your caller's time is as important as your own. Check back with him or her every 20 or 30 seconds. It is only common courtesy to provide periodic status reports. However, there is really no excuse for leaving anyone on hold for long periods. If you can't help a person within a reasonable time, offer to call back.

When you transfer a call, always tell the caller the extension number first in case you are disconnected during the transfer. Don't put the call through without briefing the person to whom the call is being transferred. This gives the recipient of the call an opportunity to prepare for the needs and temperament of the caller. It also saves the caller the time and frustration of having to repeat his or her question or explanation.

WHEN YOU ARE THE CALLER

Don't you resent it when a caller who has dialed a wrong number just slams the phone down in your ear without a simple, "I'm sorry?" Remember that, when you are the one who dials the wrong number.

Hanging up without an apology is not only rude — it can be bad for business. Don't assume that just because the person on the other end of the line can't see you, he won't know who you are. Technology has made it possible to trace many calls by simply pressing a few buttons on the keypad. Many people now have devices that automatically display the phone numbers of all incoming calls.

Before you place any call, get yourself organized. Know what you want to say and to accomplish. If you will be referring to certain materials, have them ready. If the other person will also need these materials, send or fax them ahead of time.

Never assume that people will recognize your voice, no matter how often you call or how well you know them. Immediately identify yourself to whoever answers the phone. If an assistant answers, give your complete name and the name of your company. Repeat this information when the client or customer answers, in case the assistant hasn't relayed it completely and accurately.

It is impolite to walk into someone's office without being invited, and the same is true for "dropping in" via the telephone. Briefly explain the purpose of your call and ask if the person has time to talk to you now. If he or she is busy at the moment, ask when would be a better time to call back.

Know when and how to say goodbye. When you have concluded your business, close with a brief summary of how you plan to follow up: "I'll have that proposal to you on Monday." End with a positive statement, such as "It's been nice to talk to you." Then say goodbye and gently hang up the phone (no slamming, please). Never make any comments to anyone in your work area until after you have hung up. The other person may still be on the line.

SPEAKERPHONES

Speakerphones can be a great way to bring a group of people together for a conversation. However, be sure to let the person on the other end of the line know when you're using the speakerphone and immediately announce who is present in the room. If someone enters the room during the conversation, inform whoever is on the telephone right away. If someone is going to hear what they say, it is only fair and polite to let people know. Speakerphones should be avoided unless it is a conference call.

Avoid putting your voice mail on speakerphone, it's annoying to others who can hear it throughout the hallway and it could be embarrassing to the person who left the voice-mail message.

CELL PHONES

Many people are using these phones in a way that endangers themselves and everyone around them. Cell phones were simply not made for chatting with friends as you're driving down the highway at 55 miles an hour.

Whenever possible, wait until you are parked or stopped in traffic before using your cell phone. You can't focus your full attention on driving when you are talking on the phone. There is also no way you can fully focus on a conversation while trying to negotiate your way through rush-hour traffic.

Dialing a number while driving is particularly unsafe. Pre-program the numbers you call most often. If you need to jot something down regarding a conversation, pull over or use a dictation device. Never try to write while you are driving.

Let the other person know you are in the car at the very beginning of your conversation. Then if you start to fade in and out or are suddenly disconnected, the person will understand why. As with any telephone conversation, try to eliminate as much background noise as you can. Roll up the windows, turn off the radio, and lower the air conditioning. Speak loudly and clearly.

Always get permission before calling someone else's cell phone. A ringing telephone can be a dangerous distraction to someone who is driving. You don't know where they are or what kind of traffic situation they are negotiating.

Also, all incoming cell phone calls are billed to the recipient. Also avoid making calls in public areas like theaters, restaurants, transportation, meetings, and elevators. The technology is a wonderful way to stay connected, however, when it interferes with others, it is just plain rude. If you must use them publicly, keep your voice low. Consider turning it off if you are any place that the ringing would disturb others. Cell phones should be turned off in public places like theaters, movies, transportation, restaurants, meetings, presentations, etc.

VOICE-MAIL COURTESY

When you dictate a message on someone's voice mail, you want to create just as professional an impression as if you had visited his or her office:

- Keep the message brief — prepare, so you don't ramble.

- Speak slowly and enunciate clearly.

- Give your name and phone number at both the beginning of the message and at the end.

- Listen to the message you leave and rerecord it if necessary.

When you record an outgoing message to greet callers on your own voice-mail system, be courteous and cheerful. Provide your callers with accurate information for reaching you at another time or place, or give them an idea of when you'll return their calls.

BEEPERS & PAGERS

When they are activated in public places, beepers and pagers are annoying to others. Try to use them only when it is absolutely necessary and, if possible, keep pagers on vibrate mode. When you answer your page, go to a private place to carry on your conversation.

PRIVACY

EIGHT

While taking the train to New York one day, and trying to work, I couldn't concentrate because there were two men sitting behind me using cell phones. The one was talking about his sex life — more than anyone in the train would, or should, want to know. The other man was giving insider stock information. Of course, everyone around him, myself included, was listening to that conversation!

Why were these two men so oblivious? Often people are so preoccupied or self-absorbed, they forget to consider their surroundings. They hold conversations or use their cell phones in public places.

All too frequently, inside information, gossip about people's affairs, performance appraisals, and other confidential or sensitive information is inadvertently overheard by people who should not be hearing it.

Be especially careful not to hold private conversations in the following eight places:

1) Planes, trains and automobiles

Two businessmen were on a plane, heading to give a

final presentation for a very large contract. On the flight, they discussed their strategy and practiced their presentation. They knew that the decision was between their firm and one other company. The businessmen gave their presentation, and felt they had done well. Several days later, when they called the prospect to ask who got the contract, they were told a third company won the bid. They voiced surprise — they didn't realize there was another competitor. Apparently, sitting behind them on the airplane for the entire flight was this third competitor, who overhead their strategy. He called the prospect, was able to set up an appointment, and won the million-dollar contract.

2) Elevators
3) Hallways
4) Cubicles

**"Hey, let's discuss the details
of the confidential merger."**

5) Restrooms

Talking about other people or making disparaging comments about work while in a company's bathroom or any other public area is always risky and poor etiquette — besides, who knows who may be on the other side of the stall listening?

I once walked into a bathroom and heard two women complaining that they were attending training. They didn't want to hear any more about hand washing. They didn't know who I was — a business trainer, professional speaker and author on books about etiquette — and I didn't know if they were in my etiquette program that day, but I quickly went into a stall and waited until they left before leaving. As I walked to my training room, I held my breath hoping they wouldn't be there and feel embarrassed by recognizing me. Fortunately they weren't — the women were attending a different class.

6) Company cafeteria
7) Restaurants
8) Other public transportation (taxis or buses)

Be particularly careful about your privacy when using a cell phone. E-mail, voice mail and faxes are not truly private either. Unless your message can appear in *The Wall Street Journal* or *USA Today,* you should be mindful of what you say and where you say it.

Be careful if you use a laptop on public transportation or in a park. Whoever is sitting next to you can usually see everything you are typing.

In short, be careful. Information spread by word of mouth or by technology can be dangerous. You have to protect the privacy of your clients and colleagues as well as your own.

TODAY'S TECHNOLOGY
Today, no matter what business you are in, you will

depend heavily on technology. It is amazing how frequently people forget that other people are affected whenever technology is being used.

Here is a concise summary of the guidelines for using technology with discretion:

CELL PHONE
- Do not use a cell phone in public places where it will disturb others (in meetings, on elevators, in restaurants, at the theatre).

- Remember that the wires aren't private.

- Don't call anyone on his or her cell phone without permission.

- If you use one when driving, pull over or use a speakerphone. You need to keep your hands on the wheel and your eyes on the road.

SPEAKERPHONE
- Only use one if you are on a conference call.

- Let people know who else is in the room if you or they are on a speakerphone.

- Don't use a speakerphone to listen to your voice mail if other people can overhear it.

CONFERENCE CALL
- Each person should identify himself or herself when speaking.

- If you leave the room, let others know.

• One person should act as a meeting leader.

VOICE MAIL
• Change your outgoing message regularly to let people know when you will be available.

• When you leave a message, say your name and number slowly at both the beginning and end of the message.

• Don't say it is urgent unless it is.

• Be specific and concise — no rambling.

• Remember that voice mail is not private.

E-MAIL
• Always use the subject line.

• Be concise.

• Check spelling, punctuation and grammar.

• Re-read every letter carefully before pressing "send."

• Before sending attachments, make sure the receiver will be able to access them. Check that he or she has the necessary software to view the attached file and knows how to download the attachment.

• Remember that e-mail isn't private.

   In a business setting, it's not wise to receive or send personal e-mails — even if it's interoffice e-mails. Many people might have access to your outgoing and incoming messages.
   A classic example of how this can backfire is at a small company I know. Two people were dating in this company.

After awhile, the man broke up with the woman. She wrote him a hysterical interoffice e-mail. He decided to read his e-mail when he was working at a different area of the company with a team of coworkers. Before he had a chance to look at the screen and read the new e-mail he had opened, the man was suddenly called away from the area and everyone he was with saw the hysterical e-mail from his ex-girlfriend.

FAX

• Include a cover page that indicates the number of pages being sent and a phone number.

• Call to alert the receiver that a fax is coming.

• Check spelling, punctuation, and grammar before sending the fax.

• Remember, as with e-mails, that faxes are not private.

A perfect case study that illustrates this is faxing to hotels. I travel a great deal in my business. Hotels have shared with me some of the faxes they have received for guests. One time a traveling employee was fired through a fax — and this had to be hand-delivered by an unfortunate porter! Another instance of poor fax etiquette was when a hotel received a fax that contained a lot of inside information — highly sensitive — for a company representative staying at the facility. The entire hotel staff had a chance to see this information. Who knows what might have happened. Never fax classified information or sensitive information — a better method would be to FedEx or UPS it in a sealed envelope.

BEEPER/PAGER

• Unless you are alone, put it on "vibrate" so it won't bother others.

VISITORS

Whether you are hosting a visitor or are the guest at someone else's office, you want to put your best foot forward from the very start. If a visit begins on a sour note, you may find yourself spending more time trying to repair the damage than accomplishing the real purpose of the visit.

The rules of business visiting etiquette are essentially the same as those for social visiting. For the host, it all boils down to gracious attention to your visitor's comfort. For the visitor, it requires consideration for the host's space and property. For both, it means respect for one another's time.

LATENESS

No matter what your status, position or objectives, chronic or unexplained lateness is unacceptable. Lateness never makes you seem more powerful or important. Rather, it demonstrates a disregard for the other person's time and suggests that you are not professional enough to manage your own time effectively.

Unfortunately, even the most scrupulously organized host may occasionally run a few minutes behind. If this happens, make sure your visitor is informed that the wait will be brief. Be certain the visitor has been offered comfortable seating, some reading material and, if possible, a beverage.

If you find that you will be unavoidably detained for a longer period, let your visitor know immediately. Give him or her the choice of waiting or rescheduling the visit. Apologize for the inconvenience.

HANDLING VISITORS IN YOUR OFFICE

Once the visitor has been shown into your office, offer him or her a seat. Come out from behind your desk to shake hands and greet the visitor. A desk can be an intimidating physical and psychological barrier to a guest. If possible, arrange the seating so you are sitting next to each other. If there is no room in your office for side-by-side seating, you can place your own chair directly beside your desk to remove the sense of a barrier.

As host, it is your responsibility to open the conversation unless the visitor is the one who initiated the meeting. A little bit of small talk about the traffic, weather, or some other general subject usually helps to break the ice.

Make the visitor your first priority. Emergencies may arise from time to time, but interruptions for non-urgent phone calls or office "drop ins" should not be permitted. If you must take a phone call, keep it brief. If someone comes into your office with an urgent matter, introduce your guest.

When you have finished your business, the visit still isn't over. It doesn't end until your guest has left the premises. Walking your guest to the reception area is more than polite — it eliminates the possibility that he or she will get lost. Before parting, shake hands and thank the guest for coming.

**Bob's visit fell on Chaos Day
at the branch office.**

VISITING OTHERS

"A funny thing happened to me on the way to our meeting." Whatever your reason for being late it had better be an excellent one, because — as most people realize — lateness can almost always be avoided with a little pre-planning and organization.

First, when you set the date and time for a meeting, consider how that appointment fits into the rest of your day. Don't schedule back-to-back meetings at opposite ends of the city. Leave yourself some breathing room between appointments to allow for delays or other unforeseen problems. When you are visiting someplace new, allow extra time in case you get lost. If your destination is in a heavily traveled area, leave additional time in case you are delayed by traffic jams or are forced to find an alternate route.

For an early morning appointment, have all necessary materials ready to go the night before. For later appointments, organize your materials first thing in the morning, before the demands of the workday distract you.

If you find that you are going to be more than 10 minutes late, call your host immediately. Offer the option of rescheduling. When you arrive, apologize for the delay and the inconvenience. Show respect for your host's space. Don't grab the first available chair. Wait until the host indicates where you should sit. If he or she forgets to do this, ask.

Don't shift any furniture without asking permission. Never put anything on your host's desk. Your briefcase or purse belongs on the floor beside your chair.

Although a gracious host will minimize interruptions, he or she may have to take an urgent call or respond to a co-worker's important question during the course of your visit. If someone else enters the room, stand. In the case of the phone call, indicate through body language that you are willing to step outside to allow your host to speak privately.

Be sensitive to your host's body language and other clues that suggest when it's time to leave. If you need more time to conclude your business, give your host the option of scheduling a follow-up meeting.

When it's time to say goodbye, shake hands and thank your host for his or her time. Follow up with a thank-you note, if one is appropriate.

WRITTEN COMMUNICATION

TEN

When a company sent out a mass mailing to market a new service it offered, several nasty replies from prospects came back indicating that they would never use the firm's services. One reason noted was that the handwriting on the front of the envelope looked as if a first grader did it. Also, the color of ink used did not match the marketing materials.

Writing does more than communicate ideas; it confers importance. Whenever you want to make something official, put it in writing. The written word has permanence. Written records provide documentation — a "paper trail" — to help you keep a complete and lasting record of transactions, agreements, and other important information.

Many people who are perfectly comfortable communicating their thoughts face to face or over the phone freeze when confronted with paper and pen or a computer keyboard. Yet, even in this age of cell phones, voice mail, and beepers, writing is an essential skill for every business professional.

GENERAL WRITING ETIQUETTE

You may be relieved to know that effective business

71

writing is really more a matter of good organization than of literary talent. Following three simple steps will help you to write an effective letter, memo, agenda or thank-you note:

1. First determine whether writing is appropriate. Every company has its own guidelines. Knowing when to write is as important as knowing how, so learn your company's protocol and try to follow it. Decide whether a phone call or personal visit would be more appropriate in terms of time or your company's usual procedure.

It's almost always best to write in the following cases:

- when you are expressing thanks

- when you want to clarify or confirm a phone conversation, a plan of action, or an agreement

- when you are asking someone to study a matter before reaching a conclusion or taking action

2. Organize your thoughts. Spend a few minutes organizing your thoughts before you start writing. This will spare you a lot of frustration and rewriting. First, think about the person to whom you are writing. Decide exactly what you want to say and what you want the outcome of the communication to be. What is the central point you want to make?

3. Be clear and concise. Once you begin to write, get to the point as quickly as possible. Then use the rest of your letter, memo, or whatever, to support your central thought. Don't waste your reader's time or try his or her patience with unnecessary data or verbiage. Keep your language simple and your format brief. Don't make the reader work to figure out what you're trying to say. Read what

you have written and eliminate any extra words. If there are certain things you want to particularly emphasize, it is OK to underline them or use boldface type. But don't overdo it.

THANK-YOU NOTES

If the last time you wrote a thank-you note was to thank your aunt for a present you got when you were 8 years old — and if you only wrote then because your mother forced you — shame on you!

Thank-you notes are more than good manners; they are good business. A thank-you note can be an important public relations tool. Not only does it demonstrate how gracious you are, it also shows that you value and appreciate other people.

A few well-chosen words of thanks can add a personal touch to a business relationship. It shows the recipient that you're a professional who follows things up and pays attention to details.

"Alice, someone from accounting just came by to give you a big Thank You."

A written thank you is not only appropriate when you receive a gift. It is also the right thing to do on other occasions. Here are just a few of them:

- Following a meal with a client, prospect or vendor, or a visit to someone's home. Include the person's spouse, if appropriate.

- Following a job interview or sales call. Here, the thank-you note serves two purposes. In addition to thanking the interviewer or prospect for his or her time, use it to restate your interest in the job or in serving the client or customer.

- To thank your host after a business trip. Be sure to send this as soon as possible after your return.

- To praise an employee or vendor for a job exceptionally well done. A verbal thank you may be nice, but a written thank you is much more substantial. A note is also useful in that it can be added to the recipient's personnel file.

For maximum impact, you should send any thank-you note within 24 hours. Any longer, and the recipient may wonder how appreciative you really are. Even worse, you may totally forget about your intention to write the note. But, better late than never.

Because they are more personal in nature than other forms of business communication, thank-you notes should be handwritten if at all possible. One exception would be a note following a job interview; you can type these notes to make them appear more professional. And if your penmanship leaves a great deal to be desired, you should type your notes to save your readers undue deciphering time and eyestrain. Just remember to always sign your notes by hand.

Use good quality 5 x 7 inches paper or folded note

paper. It should have your name and company name on it, but shouldn't look too formal. Do not use stationery with cute pictures; it is unprofessional.

Make sure you use the recipient's correct name and title. Never guess about the spelling, even if the name is a common one. There are a surprising number of spelling variations for even the most common names. Your closing should not be overly familiar. "Sincerely" and "Best regards" are always safe choices.

Two real-life examples of poor writing etiquette:

• Mr. or Ms.?

A letter was addressed to Jo Ellen Smith. The person who did the addressing, however, only saw the "Jo" and addressed it as "Mr." This kind of careless error could affect a client relationship.

• Spelling of company names.

One company nearly lost a new client based on an incorrect spelling of the company name — Andersen Consulting. Never assume. Always double check.

E-MAIL COURTESY

Just as all your correspondence reflects your credibility and professionalism, your e-mail also conveys an image of you.

Keep these tips in mind:

• Keep your message short.

• Don't use all capital letters. In the world of cyber communication, capital letters scream at people.

- As always, pay careful attention to your spelling and grammar.

- Remember that e-mail isn't private. Don't write anything you wouldn't want someone else to see!

- Always use a subject line, and keep it concise. It could get your message read faster.

- Always use a "sig," or "signature" file — this should contain all contact information and any tag line you may have.

- Only send copies of e-mails to those that absolutely need it.

Although you can use e-mail to send thank-you notes, it is better to hand write your message. You can e-mail other people to let them know you are pleased with someone, but actually write a note to that person.

LIVING TOGETHER IN THE WORKPLACE

ELEVEN

Y ou probably put real effort into being a good neighbor and a responsible citizen. Just as you are a member of your community and a citizen of the country you live in, you are a member of your company's staff. Along with certain rights, you also have responsibilities and obligations toward your colleagues and fellow "citizens."

Coexisting peacefully and harmoniously isn't always easy — especially when you're sharing a copier, coffee machine and conference room. But it can be done. It only requires a little common courtesy when using shared territory and equipment, and a little respect for other people's sensibilities and personal space.

EQUIPMENT ETIQUETTE

Here are seven simple rules of etiquette that apply to all office equipment:

Rule #1: If it's empty, fill it.

The coffeepot is empty again. The copier's out of toner. You need to send a fax right away, but the machine is out of paper. It's frustrating, isn't it?

Remember that feeling the next time you drink the last of the coffee, get near the end of the toner, or see that the fax paper tray is empty. Use it to make yourself a better colleague. You don't have to be Julia Child to make a pot of coffee. You don't have to be an electronic genius to know when a fax machine needs paper.

It only takes a few minutes to fill a paper tray or set up a pot of coffee. "I don't know how" is a lame excuse. Ask someone to help you.

Rule #2: If it's broken, fix it, or at least get it fixed.

Machines break down. If you happen to be around when this happens, don't just walk away and hope the next person will deal with it. Even if you didn't break it in the first place, take care of it. Quibbling about blame and responsibility is always counterproductive and totally unprofessional.

Rule #3: If you don't know how to use it properly, learn.

Misuse of equipment is more than just a time-waster. It can also damage sensitive machinery. Before you push that button or turn that dial, make sure you know exactly what you're doing.

Rule #4: If it isn't your turn, wait.

You're in a hurry. You need to use the copier right now to make 500 copies for your meeting in 10 minutes. Well get in line, because we are all in a hurry, and the person ahead of you at the machine may have a meeting in five minutes.

In the future, give yourself a little more time. If you work in a busy office, you are bound to run into a traffic jam occasionally at some critical machine.

Of course, if you are running a large job and someone needs to make a few copies, it's common courtesy to let him or her use the machine. Next time, the person who needs just a few copies might be you.

Rule #5: If it isn't yours, don't read it.

If you find someone else's document in the copy machine or see a transmission addressed to your co-worker in the fax machine, resist the temptation to gather some inside information or juicy gossip by reading it. Once you determine to whom the original belongs or to whom the fax is addressed, put the document in his or her mailbox.

The "don't read it" rule also applies to data displayed on someone else's computer screen, and to mail lying on someone else's desk.

Rule #6: If you make a mess, clean it up.

Pick up your own trash and wipe up your own spills. Take all your originals and other papers with you when you leave an area.

Rule #7: When you're finished with it, make sure it's ready for the next person to use.

Reset the copier to the standard one copy, 8 1/2 x 11 inches size. Don't change computer programming or automatic dial numbers on the fax machine without permission.

In addition to these seven basic rules that apply to all equipment, each type of machinery has its own specific etiquette considerations.

FAX MACHINES
Equipment etiquette doesn't only apply within your

office. Your courtesy should extend to the people on the receiving end of your transmissions. Don't send unsolicited faxes. Many people view them as even worse than junk mail because they waste paper and tie up valuable machine time.

Avoid sending faxes during peak hours. Whenever possible, choose times when usage is generally lighter — early in the morning, during lunch, or after official working hours. Off-peak transmissions will also save your company money if you are faxing long distance.

Never send restricted-access materials without obtaining prior permission. You cannot always be sure that the person who retrieves the message will be the one to whom you have addressed it. It might be picked up by an assistant or by whoever happens to see the fax arrive. This is also true when you fax to hotels.

Make sure your cover sheet is complete and coherent. A fax cover sheet should include the name, department, fax number, and phone number of both the recipient and the sender; the time and date sent; the number of pages; any message; and whether or not the delivery is urgent.

If the recipient uses a shared fax machine, call and give notice when you've sent a transmission.

COPIERS

Even if company policy allows you to use the copier for personal use, don't do so during peak usage hours. If you're running a large personal job, don't use up the company's paper; bring your own. As mentioned above, if you are running any large job and someone only needs a few copies, it is common courtesy to let him or her briefly interrupt you.

SHARING SPACE WITH OTHER PEOPLE

Unless you work in a one-person office, you'll need to observe certain procedures when it comes to sharing space with co-workers. Most of the "rules" in this area are simple, common sense, courtesies.

SOMEONE ELSE'S SPACE

No matter how closely people live or work together, all employees need a place to call their own. While offices, desks and file cabinets are officially company property, they are temporarily "owned" by the people who use them and should be treated accordingly.

Just as you wouldn't walk into someone's home unannounced, you shouldn't walk into anyone's office without knocking. Even if the door is open, wait until the person invites you in. If the person is on the telephone, wait until he or she is finished.

Cubicles present their own problems when it comes to privacy. Avoid barging into someone's cubicle, and don't linger around when they are on the phone. Keep your voice down when meeting in a cubicle or when on the phone. Avoid shouting across cubicles to the person over the "wall."

Think twice before playing new voice-mail messages on speaker phone. One time someone I know was quite embarrassed when a young coworker who had been on a date with another coworker played a voice mail he received on speaker phone — only several cubicles down. The message talked about the sex these two coworkers had on a date the night before.

You should also ask permission before borrowing, moving, or using any equipment in a person's office. If the other person isn't present when you use the equipment, make sure you put everything back the way you found it after you're finished. Remember, pens, papers, etc., may be company property, but don't take them from someone else's desk.

SHARED SPACE

The copy room, conference room, cafeteria and restrooms don't belong to any one person. So who is responsible for keeping them in good condition?

You are, along with everybody else who uses them. This doesn't have to be a big deal. In most cases, it's just a matter of cleaning up after yourself.

Sometimes a bit of pre-planning is required. For instance, if you want to use the conference room, you may have to schedule it in advance. This benefits you as much as anyone else, as it ensures that you won't find it already taken when you are ready to begin your meeting.

Find out the proper scheduling procedures and follow them. Be as flexible as you possibly can. If a conflict occurs, try to resolve it calmly, politely and discreetly. Also, leave the meeting room clean — don't make a mess.

Smoking in shared spaces can present etiquette problems for both the smokers and the non-smokers in a building. Many offices now provide non-smoking areas and some are completely smoke-free. Ignoring your company's smoking policy is more than bad manners. It demonstrates a lack of respect for authority and a disregard for your co-workers' health. If you're not sure about company policy, ask. In any case, always ask permission from the individuals you are with at the time.

YOUR OWN SPACE

Although you are the one who inhabits it, your office, cubicle or desk area is more than just an expression of your personality. It is also a reflection of your company. Personal items can make your office feel more comfortable and homey, but be sure that they are all in good taste and fit your company's protocol for decorations. Make sure your space is always neat and organized. You never know who's going to be passing by or stopping in.

OPENING DOORS

Once upon a time, it was considered proper etiquette for a man to open the door for a woman. It still is. However, today it's just as proper for a woman to open the door for a man.

The deciding factor in determining who opens the door, goes through it first, or holds it open for someone else, is not gender, corporate status, or age. The determining factor should always be good old common courtesy. Under ordinary circumstances (i.e. no one involved is on crutches), the first person to arrive at the door should be the one to open it and proceed through it first. When this is you, be sure to hold the door open until the next person is able to grab it. Allowing a door to slam in someone's face is rude and dangerous. If someone needs help, offer it.

These are the guidelines that apply in today's working world, but for some people, old habits and traditional etiquette practices die hard. If a man insists on holding the door for a woman, chances are he truly believes he is doing the correct thing. A polite and professional woman will not view this act as a challenge to her independence and physical capabilities. She won't launch into a tirade on the equality of women in the workplace. Embarrassing another person is never good manners. Appreciate the gracious intent of the gesture. Smile. And don't forget to say "thank you."

It is no longer necessary for men to allow women to get off elevators first. Whoever is closest to the door should exit first. When waiting for an elevator (train or bus), move off to the side so the people who are exiting can get off; then enter.

PROCRASTINATION

Although procrastination is really an undesirable work habit rather than bad manners, rudeness can be a serious side effect. A tendency to procrastinate can severely hurt your ability to work well with those around you. If co-workers are counting on you to get work done, any unanticipated delay or failure to complete your part can cause them great difficulty and stress. It can hurt their project and damage their reputation, along with yours. Procrastination can harm your business relationships and lose you the respect of others.

If you have this problem, you should address it immediately. If you don't, the costs in missed opportunities, increased anxiety, and broken relationships can be devastating. Here are some tried-and-true steps for avoiding procrastination:

1. Look at the task in its entirety. Find a motivation to complete it: helping others, making a sale, keeping a job.

2. Break the task into small, manageable chunks.

3. Establish a time frame for completing each chunk. Be realistic.

4. Post the task on things you will look at often, such as your day timer, computer, telephone, and bathroom mirror.

5. As you complete each chunk, give yourself a reward.

Procrastination is really a form of fear, and it indicates a lack of confidence. Give yourself positive messages about your ability to get things done. An "I can do it now" philosophy says to everyone around you, "I believe in myself." In time, you will create new habits that eliminate procrastination.

HANDLING CRITICISM &
COMPLIMENTS GRACEFULLY

An administrative assistant I know received a thank-you note from a sales rep at a company because she spent extra time and helped him with a special project. When I asked the result of that thank-you note, she said, "I'll do his work again before I do anyone else's."

Thank-you notes are a form of compliment and can only help you in the business world. The offering of compliments and criticisms must always be handled with extreme grace and tact. You want every compliment you give to sound sincere. When you offer feedback, you want to be constructive and to be sure your suggestions are understood, but you don't want to sound defensive or confrontational. When you are on the receiving end of compliments or criticisms, you want to respond graciously and appropriately.

OFFERING FEEDBACK

It often seems as if everyone is a critic, even you. While accepting or giving criticism is rarely viewed as pleasant, it doesn't have to be negative or hurtful. It can and should be helpful. It has to be given — and taken — in the right manner.

Unsolicited feedback can provoke a negative or hostile

response from the recipient. As always, think twice before you speak. Before offering feedback to anyone, be sure that you have both the authority and a solid reason for doing it. If, after careful consideration, you decide that your feedback is warranted and appropriate, you must still keep in mind that criticism is a bitter pill for many people to swallow.

If handled correctly, the giving and accepting of constructive criticism can actually increase your professional credibility and status. Here are three tips for making your feedback as palatable and valuable as possible:

- Be tactful.

- Be specific.

- Be accurate.

It is best to take a positive and constructive approach. Telling someone, "You did a lousy job" accomplishes nothing beyond making him or her feel demoralized and defensive. It may be accurate, but it is not tactful, and it isn't specific enough to be helpful. You haven't let the person know what he or she did wrong or offered any suggestions for improvement. Typically, people respond to this kind of criticism with embarrassment, denial, or even outright hostility. A better approach would be something like this: "The estimates in this proposal should include a more comprehensive advertising budget."

Focus on the behavior you hope to change, not on the person. Insults, name-calling, and personal attacks are never warranted or acceptable, no matter what the circumstances. Avoid "you" statements, which sound like an attack, such as "You really let me down." "You" statements always make someone feel defensive. Remember that in all probability, the person really wants to do the right thing. However, it isn't always easy for others to meet your expectations, particularly if they aren't sure exactly what they are.

If possible, mention some of the person's positive skills and contributions along with your specific suggestions for improvement. For example: "The research you did for this report is very thorough. In the future, please remember to use the spell-checker. There are four misspelled words."

Always choose an appropriate time and a private location for offering criticism. No one will appreciate being embarrassed in public. Don't choose the middle of a staff meeting or an encounter at the coffee machine, where your conversation is likely to be overheard by others.

After offering a verbal criticism, it is often a good idea to follow up in writing. Today, many companies require a written follow-up to provide a record of the interaction and to ensure that the individual understands the key points and recommendations.

The woman who does my public relations told me horror stories about how one of her former bosses would criticize employees. This woman was the editor at a pharmaceutical publication. When a staff member did something that this editor deemed wrong, she would raise her voice, get red in the face and neck, and literally scream at the person who made the mistake. Not only did the editor overreact to various circumstances, she would offer this feedback in the middle of the office, in full view and hearing of all staff members. Often, the subjects of her frequent rants ended up in tears. Needless to say, the turnover rate at this publication was high. Even when this woman had her friendly moments, and offered compliments, everyone in the office still walked on eggshells, waiting for her to snap.

"Come on in, Ted, so I can thank you for your 'brutally honest' critique."

RECEIVING FEEDBACK

Everyone finds himself or herself on the receiving end of criticism from time to time. When this happens, the most important thing is to remain calm and fight the natural instinct to become paranoid or defensive. Here are five tips that can help you to handle criticism and turn it into a positive learning experience.

1. Listen. Keep an open mind. Everyone makes mistakes, and we can all use improvement in some areas. Resist the temptation to argue or make excuses.

2. Consider the source. Does the person speaking have the authority, knowledge, and expertise to give you this feedback? Does he or she have an ulterior motive? (Be careful not to invent one, though, just to make yourself feel better.)

3. Ask for specific examples. Don't accept generalities such as "poor," "disappointing," or "lousy." Politely ask the speaker to tell you exactly what is wrong. Questions like, "Exactly what was wrong with the presentation" or a request such as, "Help me to understand what you mean by 'poor'" should help you to get some useful information.

4. Evaluate the criticism. If it is valid, accept it gracefully and with a positive attitude. Tell the speaker you appreciate his or her comments and be enthusiastic about your willingness and ability to use the suggestions to improve your performance.

5. Keep the useful information, but let go of the negative feelings. Don't dwell on the embarrassment of being criticized. Hold your head up high and move on.

GIVING COMPLIMENTS

Everyone needs to feel appreciated. A word of praise can do wonders for any employee's spirit and motivation.

You don't have to gush over someone to express your appreciation. A simple "Good job — keep up the good work" is enough to make most people feel good. The amount and specific wording of your praise should suit your personality. Low-key praise is perfectly fine, as long as it's sincere.

Some people hesitate to compliment employees because they worry that the praise will "go to their heads." To avoid that possibility, simply be specific and focus your praise on the particular action or accomplishment rather than on the person in general. For example, you might say, "The way you organized that report made it very easy for the client to read and understand," rather than, "You're really terrific." The former is more useful, too.

Increase the impact of your praise by giving it in writing or in public, whenever possible and appropriate. Put a copy of any complimentary notes or memos in your employee's permanent personnel file.

If you have something nice to say, don't wait. If you don't say it right away, chances are you will forget. Besides, according to the principles of behavior modification, the sooner you reinforce positive behavior, the more likely it is to be repeated.

RECEIVING COMPLIMENTS

A little humility is a good thing. But too much can be as detrimental to your image as too little.

It is not arrogant or immodest to accept a compliment, as long as you do it gracefully. In fact, false modesty is not only unbecoming, but can be downright insulting to the judgment of the person who paid you the compliment.

"Thank you" is always a polite and correct way to acknowledge a compliment. Don't add, "It was nothing" or some other qualifying statement that diminishes you and your accomplishment. However, it's always appropriate to acknowledge others who were instrumental in your success: "I couldn't have done it without Sally and Ted," or to share something valuable you learned from the experience: "Researching that area was great for me. I learned so much about the pre-teen market."

Once, after an annual team meeting at a large company, I asked the officer who put together the whole affair if she got any thank-you notes. She said two — one from the managing director, one from the senior vice president. How is it that they were the only two people to take the time to acknowledge the work that was done? Also, at this same event, 50 people showed up without having RSVPed. Consequently, they were short of food. Poor etiquette to say the least.

COPING WITH CONFLICT

No matter how hard we try, we cannot totally avoid conflict. In fact, sometimes trying too hard to avoid it allows a disagreement that could have been settled with a few well-chosen words to erupt into an all-out war.

The trick is to deal with conflicts before they escalate. This does not mean expressing every criticism or complaint that comes into your mind. It simply means identifying meaningful areas of disagreement and trying to resolve them calmly, reasonably and politely.

Whenever two people disagree on how to handle a particular situation, the potential for conflict exists. You may experience disputes over such everyday matters as office space, work distribution or status. Whatever the source of potential conflict, the best ways to handle it are:

- Think before you speak. Focus on the specific behavior or situation that's at the root of the problem. Generalizations and personal attacks solve nothing. They only create more conflict and, in the end, nobody wins.

- Ask yourself, "Is it worth it?" Some things such as a desk or parking space may not be worth arguing over. Choose your fights carefully. You don't want to be viewed as petty or overbearing. Besides, a gracious concession every once in a while can show people how reasonable and professional you are and win you respect and good will.

- Go straight to the source. Nobody likes someone who runs to "the boss" with every little thing. One sign of a professional is the ability to solve your own problems. Approach the person with whom you have the problem in private. Try to arrange for a meeting on neutral ground — somewhere other than your office or his or hers.

- Keep your temper under control. Don't let anger get the better of you. Don't attack the person with "you" statements or resort to name-calling.

- Be assertive, not aggressive. These are very different things. Assertiveness is strong and professional; aggressiveness is overbearing and threatening. For example, if someone confronts you with a topic you don't wish to discuss right then, you should say so, but in an assertive, not nasty or aggressive, manner. Simply and calmly say, "I'm not comfortable discussing this now. I'd like to postpone it until our next meeting." This should be enough to get the message across quite clearly.

- Control the volume and pitch of your voice. Keep them calm and steady. Watch your body language. Maintain eye contact. Don't cross you arms or point your finger aggressively.

- Be open-minded. Listen to the other person's side of the story. Often, understanding the motivation behind a particular behavior will give you a clue as to a fair and mutually acceptable solution.

- Stay focused. If there are several issues involved, address each one separately. Don't combine them all into one big "You're out to get me" issue.

- Be flexible. Try to work out solutions together. Listen to the other person's suggestions, make sure you understand them, then make your own. When you reach a conclusion on an issue, restate it to confirm the agreement.

- Follow through. Be prepared to stick to your end of the agreement. If the other person doesn't, offer a polite reminder. If necessary, put the agreement in writing.

- If all else fails. If you absolutely cannot come to a mutually acceptable conclusion, then you should consider taking the problem to a higher authority within the company. Resort to this only if the matter is truly important and if all attempts at working it out between you have failed.

OFFENSIVE BEHAVIOR

It is important to add that no one should ever be expected to put up with off-color, sexist, racist, or other offensive comments or behavior. Don't apologize or explain your reaction. A simply stated, "I'm offended by that" should get your point across.

WHEN A COLLEAGUE BEHAVES BADLY

What happens when you keep your temper, but a co-worker doesn't? You think before you speak, refrain from acting aggressive, and try to discuss the disagreement calmly, but your colleague doesn't act in kind. He or she attacks you, raises his or her voice, hurls accusations, or goes behind your back.

Unfortunately, there is not too much we can do when someone else behaves poorly. We are all faced with this kind of adversity at times. When we are, it's our attitude that can make a difference.

It isn't fun when people "lose it" and subject us to hostility, sarcasm or back-stabbing. But we don't have to join them in their unfortunate mode of behavior. We can maintain our professionalism and self-respect, remaining calm and staying within the guidelines of good business etiquette.

Instead of getting angry, try to find some value in adversity. Ask yourself, "What did I learn from this? What can I do differently? How can I help other people in similar situations?"

LOOK AT YOURSELF

Sometimes we're so busy observing everyone else's imperfect behavior that we fail to recognize our own shortcomings. To avoid becoming the source of conflict, make sure you think before you speak, and that your behavior demonstrates sensitivity to the people and situations around you.

Do you refer to women as "girls" or a particular ethnic or religious group as "you people?" Don't. Make sure you know the correct terms of address to avoid offending or insulting anyone.

Do you automatically group everyone of a particular gender, ethnicity, or religious affiliation into a single category with shared characteristics and behaviors? For instance, if a woman is having a bad day, do you automatically assume that her hormones are the cause? Don't. Every person is an individual and should be treated as one.

Do you believe that the only correct viewpoint on a topic is the one you hold? There is no one more irritating than the person who thinks he or she knows it all. Learn to listen and respect other people's points of view. Each of us has things to learn from other people.

Etiquette comes down to having respect for yourself and for others. If life is a journey, then being kind and respectful of others is one way to help sweeten it.

MEETING & PRESENTATIONS

FOURTEEN

When a group of consultants met with their clients in a conference room setting, one consultant pulled out his nail clipper and started clipping his nails.

When you speak in front of a group, you communicate as much about yourself as about the topic at hand. What this consultant illustrated is poor manners. Each meeting opportunity is a chance to demonstrate your professionalism, interpersonal skills and effectiveness.

LEADING A MEETING

Research indicates that people in middle management spend an average of 35 percent of their workweek in meetings. In upper management, the average climbs even higher, to 50 percent.

However, not all of these meetings are necessary, efficient or productive. Before opting to call a meeting, think carefully about whether one is really necessary. Sometimes you can accomplish as much — or more — with a simple action like a telephone call, letter or e-mail.

If you determine that a meeting is necessary, then you are responsible for planning it. Careful planning is crucial if you want to accomplish anything. It also reassures the participants that you didn't call a meeting to take up their time unnecessarily. In other words, planning is an important courtesy.

To map out a productive meeting, you can use a technique followed by journalists. Reporters who need to make sure all bases are covered have traditionally used the "5 Ws and an H" — "Who, What, When, Where, Why and How." Addressing all six questions ensures that every aspect of a story is presented. We put these elements in a different order: Why, Who, Where, What, How and When — to cover all the bases in planning a meeting.

- **Why?** Why are you calling the meeting? Begin by outlining exactly what you hope to accomplish.

- **Who?** Decide whom to invite, asking only as many participants as necessary. If the objective of your meeting is to present information or to motivate your staff, the numbers will be greater than if the purpose is to discuss or solve a problem. A good guideline is that the more give-and-take there will be, the fewer participants you should include.

- **Where?** Make arrangements for the facilities. Choose a space large enough to accommodate the number of participants, but not so large that seeing or hearing becomes difficult. Arrange for any equipment and refreshments you would like.

- **What?** What will be covered? Plan an agenda detailing the topics and the order in which they will be discussed. For long meetings, schedule short breaks every 90 minutes so people can stretch their legs and clear their heads. Keep breaks to seven to nine minutes. Longer ones make it harder to get everyone reassembled and settled down.

It is a good idea to discuss the agenda with the participants before you finalize it. This way, you are less likely to be delayed or sidetracked by proposed changes and additions during the actual meeting. Try to give the agenda to participants two or three days in advance. Include any other materials that are pertinent to the meeting.

• **How?** Establish some ground rules to make sure the meeting flows smoothly. Be firm about enforcing them. The rules should help discourage interruptions, rude or disruptive behavior, and filibustering. They should encourage the sharing of information, listening, and using the time productively.

• **When?** If possible, it's best to check with key participants before setting the date. Give participants as much advance notice as possible so they can prepare materials and gather information to bring to the meeting.

KEEPING PEOPLE INFORMED

There may be people who don't need to attend but should know that the meeting will take place and what will be discussed. You can send these people an agenda with a note promising follow-up information after the meeting. This is also a good way to keep people in the loop who ought to attend the meeting but are unable to be there.

During the meeting, the leader can act as a facilitator or there can be an actual facilitator. His or her job entails stating the objectives, guiding the discussion so it follows the agenda, enforcing the ground rules, and making sure the meeting begins and ends on time.

At the end of the meeting, it is the meeting leader's job to review and clarify any actions that are supposed to result from the meeting. Determine and verify who is responsible for what. Set deadlines with interim checkpoints.

AFTER THE MEETING

After the other participants have left the room, make sure you restore it to its proper order. Return equipment. Pick up any trash.

Within 48 hours, send out minutes. These are simply a recap of what took place at the meeting, including a list of objectives achieved, actions to be taken, the people who are responsible for those actions, any additional comments, and the date of a follow-up meeting if there will be one.

ATTENDING A MEETING: THREE "P'S"

When you're invited to attend a meeting, remember the "3 P's": preparation, punctuality and participation.

- Preparation. Ask the person planning the meeting what is expected of you. What will be your role during the meeting? What materials or information should you bring?

- Punctuality. Arrive on time. Whether you're meeting with one person or 10, making people wait is bad manners and bad for your image.

- Participation. Present your materials and ideas. Keep your comments brief and to the point. Stick to the agenda. Listen with an open mind to what others have to say. Ask questions when you need something to be clarified. Make notes on any follow-up actions you will be expected to take.

After the meeting, review the minutes and brief anyone in your department who should be aware of the results and the follow-up actions. Complete your follow-up actions on or before the deadline.

PRESENTATION SKILLS AND ETIQUETTE

Being an effective speaker takes more than just knowing

your topic. You can be the top authority in your field and still have trouble holding an audience's attention if you are not a courteous presenter.

You may wonder what courtesy has to do with a speaker's effectiveness. The answer is a great deal.

Presentation courtesy means paying attention and responding to the interests and needs of your audience. When planning a presentation, the first thing you should do is determine exactly who your audience members are. Why should they care what you have to say? What's in it for them? Based on the answers to these questions, you can begin to prepare your presentation.

Start with a one-sentence summary of your central theme. Then, organize your information and supporting materials around it. Make sure your language, materials and conclusions are easy for your audience to follow and understand. You may be offering them the key to world peace, but if your audience members are lost or asleep, they'll miss it. Illustrate key points by using real-life examples. Real examples clarify your points and make them easier to understand and remember. If appropriate, inject some humor from time to time, but never to offend anyone.

Be responsive to questions from the audience. Listen to the entire question before beginning your answer. Always paraphrase or repeat the question before answering. Keep your answer focused on the question — don't go off on tangents.

Manage your time. If you're scheduled to speak for 20 minutes, don't stretch it into a half-hour. Overtime may be exciting at sporting events, but at business presentations it only makes audiences fidgety. Practice your presentation to make sure you can fit everything you want to say into the allotted time.

But meeting etiquette also applies to the participants. I saw a presenter once who began to do her presentation for a meeting of about 50 people. Everyone had their laptop computers open. When she asked a participant why their laptops were open she was told that, "We're checking our e-mail. If you're any good, you'll see the tops of the laptops closing."

Things NOT to do during a meeting:

• conduct sidebar conversation when someone else has the "floor"

• put down others

• do a crossword puzzle or other non-meeting-related work

• talk on a cell phone

• leave a beeper on (unless it's on "vibrate" mode)

BUSINESS TRAVEL

FIFTEEN

Whether your job requires you to travel extensively or only occasionally, remember that good manners don't belong only in your home office. They must travel with you. When you are "on the road," expect the unexpected. It is often during these unanticipated moments that your business etiquette and professionalism face some of their toughest challenges.

Whatever the purpose of your business trip, the two major keys to success are preparation and flexibility. These may seem incompatible, but they're not. In fact, they are two complementary sides of the professional personality, and they are equally important.

TRAVEL TIPS

Preparation for your trip begins with focusing on its purpose. Perhaps you are visiting a client, a customer, or a prospect. Or you may be participating in contract negotiations. You may be a presenter at a conference or an attendee. Or you may be a trouble-shooter or district manager whose job requires you to cover extensive geographical territories.

Whatever your purpose, careful scheduling is crucial. This means more than just booking your airline tickets, hotel reservations and rental car. It means planning your entire itinerary in writing. Your itinerary should include the phone numbers of each place you will be as well as the dates and times of any appointments you have scheduled. Make three copies: one for you, one to leave at the office for an assistant or co-worker, and one for your family. This is not only courteous, it is a necessity if you must be reached in an emergency.

Contact anyone you need to see during your trip to coordinate your schedules. Don't risk flying all the way across the country only to find that the person you need to see is out of town. You also don't want to force your contact into making last minute schedule changes to accommodate you.

Don't wait until the last minute to prepare any documents or other materials you need to bring along. Be thorough. It can be devastating to be thousands of miles from the office and find that you've forgotten a key part of your presentation.

TIPS FOR KEEPING IT PRIVATE ON THE ROAD

The best way to protect against having sensitive information stolen or overheard when you travel on business, is to not discuss it or leave a paper trail. When taking a road trip — business or pleasure — only bring essential documents.

I know someone who has lost a coat, cell phone and other items while traveling on business. The scary thing is that this professional likes to get her mail forwarded to her when she's on a prolonged business trip. She likes getting a jump on it so it doesn't pile up in the office. A great idea. But, it's risky. What might she accidentally leave at a hotel? What might fall out her hands while she's struggling to carry her briefcase and luggage? At least her office makes it a policy not to send client checks, bank statements, or other highly sensitive information!

Remember, some people actually look to pick up corporate secrets in public places. Some underhanded professionals will even justify booking first class airfare tickets in the hopes of improving the information they can overhear, or see on a computer laptop.

If you are on public transportation (planes, buses, trains, etc.), or in public places (park, restaurant, etc.), remember that others can view your laptop computer screen. Don't work on confidential information like client materials, performance appraisals, corporate presentations, etc., if others near you can possibly see what you're doing. Try to keep to a minimum any sensitive information that you read or type. Always be alert and close documents if you notice your seatmate paying particular attention to what you're doing.

Little did Jean realize that the pigeon was working for the other guy.

PACKING

Choose your travel wardrobe with your itinerary in mind. Will you be attending a gala formal dinner or a golf tournament? Pack accordingly. Remember that even if the dress code is "casual," that means business casual — comfortable, but always professional. Pack as little as possible. Mix-and-match wardrobe pieces offer maximum versatility while taking up a minimum of space in your suitcase. Wrinkle-resistant fabrics that don't show stains as easily are the best choices.

Consider whether business gifts are appropriate. In some cultures, they are actually expected. Find out before you go.

THE UNEXPECTED SNAG

You know how to prepare for your business trip. What happens when, despite all your careful preparation, something goes awry? What if you miss your connecting flight? What if you land in Cleveland, but your luggage travels to San Diego?

This is where flexibility comes in. No matter what happens, the first thing to do is take a deep breath. Every problem has a solution. But if you're jumping up and down and hyperventilating, you're in no condition to figure one out.

A little clear thinking and a good sense of humor can help you get through just about anything. Often, the way you handle a crisis tells people more about your professionalism than they would have learned if everything had gone according to plan.

TRAVEL ETIQUETTE

Travel can be a grueling test of manners. A crowd of strangers is confined in a limited space for an extended period of time. The seating is elbow-to-elbow. Every move you make has an effect on someone else. Just about everyone, including you, is tired, and everyone, at least to some degree, is frazzled.

In the close quarters of an airplane or train, every inch of space can become fiercely coveted territory. Be conscious of which space belongs to you and which space doesn't. Don't stretch out into the aisle or sprawl onto your neighbor's seat. Don't kick the seat in front of you.

Keep your belongings within the confines of your own space. Airline regulations require you to stow carry-on luggage in overhead compartments or under your seat. The primary reason for this is safety. But it is also the polite thing to do. If you find that your luggage doesn't fit in either of these two designated places, tell a flight attendant right away. It can be checked and stored with the rest of the luggage.

Before reaching to adjust air, light, or window shades, ask your neighbor's permission. Your comfort may be another person's misery.

Small talk between passengers is often appropriate and even welcome, especially during long trips. However, your neighbor may prefer to read, sleep, work, or simply be left alone. If the person is not responsive, don't push. Find something else to do or someone else to talk to.

When traveling, be sensitive to the special needs of other people. For example, if someone has a disability or is elderly, be patient if he or she takes a few minutes longer to get settled in his or her seat. Pushing and shoving is always rude, even when you are in a hurry. It won't get you where you're going any faster. When boarding, disembarking, or getting your luggage, wait your turn.

Taxis present their own unique set of etiquette challenges. In many cities it is a feat just to get one. Like you, everyone is in a hurry, and everyone has important business.

If you visit or stay at a hotel, let the doorman, bellman or other designated staff member hail a cab for you. Not only is it proper etiquette to allow a person to do his or her job, but it is usually the quickest, most practical way to get a cab. Tip the person $1 or $2, depending on the difficulty the person had hailing the cab.

When two people are waiting in the same location to hail a cab, the general guideline is first come, first served, regardless of gender. However, either party can graciously yield, particularly if one has a pressing engagement and the other doesn't. In some cities, people also have the option of sharing a cab and its costs, even if they're going to different destinations.

When you're stuck in a traffic jam it can be irritating to watch the fare on the meter rise higher and higher even though you aren't moving. However, it's not fair to ask the driver to turn off the meter. In most cases, drivers are reimbursed in part for time and mileage.

Add an appropriate tip along to the required fare. Fifteen percent of the total fare is standard.

TRAVELING WITH A COMPANION

Traveling with your spouse or a companion can make a business trip feel more like a holiday. However, both you and your companion must always keep in mind that the first priority of the trip is business.

Time together for touring or enjoying other activities must be scheduled around business, not the other way around. Your companion must also be flexible enough to gracefully accept any sudden change in plans.

If you attend any business functions together, your companion should dress appropriately and be ready to mingle with your bosses, clients or customers, co-workers, and their spouses or significant others. Above all, there should be no griping about long meetings and jam-packed business schedules — just patience, politeness and a positive attitude.

INTERNATIONAL ETIQUETTE

SIXTEEN

This is an exciting time to be in business. Today's workplace spans the entire globe, encompassing countries and cultures that many of us have never encountered before. This globalization of business has opened up entirely new worlds of opportunity for American professionals.

At the same time, this has presented an entirely new dimension of behavioral challenges. Most of the rules and guidelines we have discussed so far have been fairly straightforward and easy to grasp. Many require only a little thought and some common sense. But each culture has its own rules, traditions and protocols. While the need for courtesy and respect is universal, the ways they are expressed is not. What is appropriate and polite in one culture may be totally inappropriate or even offensive in another.

Business professionals cannot afford to be rude, whether they are at home or abroad. Even if your faux pas was simply an honest mistake, the costs in lost business and damaged relationships can be terribly high. "I didn't know" is unlikely to repair the damage. With the wealth of guidebooks, cross-cultural reference materials, and training programs that are available today, ignorance is not a viable excuse.

WHEN YOU ARE THE GUEST

The old adage, "When in Rome, do as the Romans do" is highly relevant for the international business traveler. It is an important key to personal and professional success in a foreign country.

Whatever your purpose in visiting another country, your first job is to adapt. Before you leave home, do some research. Buy a guidebook that includes key phrases. Go to the library and check the Internet. Talk to people from the country you're planning to visit. If possible, familiarize yourself with the food of the country by visiting restaurants in the U.S. that specialize in its cuisine. Here are some basics that you should try to learn before your trip:

- appropriate greetings
- the currency system
- the dress code
- as much of the language as possible
- the usual weather conditions at the time of your visit
- gift-giving rituals
- religious beliefs and customs integral to the culture
- any important cultural events, holidays, or sporting events that will take place during your visit

Once you arrive, carefully observe the behaviors of the people who live in the country. Don't be afraid to ask questions. Asking questions shows an open mind, a willingness to learn and a desire to be respectful. Try to find a mentor or guide to help show you the lay of the land, both geographically and culturally.

Throughout your stay, make an effort to look at things from the perspective of the host culture, not from your own. Do not judge or criticize other people's manners because they don't fit American standards. Remember, your hosts are probably working equally hard not to judge or criticize your manners.

Be open to new things. Have a sense of adventure. Try the local cuisine. Use every new experience to broaden your knowledge and your horizons.

WHEN YOU ARE THE HOST

Although it's the visitor's job to adapt to the local culture, it's the duty of the gracious host to make it as easy and comfortable as possible for the visitor to do this. As host, you need to learn all you can about the visitor's culture prior to the visit. This will help you to view your own culture through his or her eyes, so you can anticipate many of the questions or problems he or she may have.

From the moment he or she arrives, your guest should feel welcome. You or someone you designate should be waiting at the airport to greet your visitor when the plane lands. Be certain that you (or the person you designate) understand and use the appropriate greeting protocol. This is a sign of respect for the visitor and the culture that he or she represents. If you don't know what constitutes an acceptable greeting in your guest's culture, find out.

Arrange for a delivery of food or flowers to the visitor's hotel room. This gesture is particularly meaningful if the gift selection is based on knowledge of the person's culture, customs and individual taste.

Invite the visitor to your home. In addition to providing a glimpse of American home life, this gesture can help to establish a bond between you and your guest.

Whether you are dining with your guest at your home or in a restaurant, be sensitive to his or her dining customs, restrictions and preferences. Never try to insist that a guest sample your favorite American delicacy. Some cultures have very strict dietary laws. Or your guest may have a personal reason for refusing.

If it's the visitor's first trip, offer to conduct a personal tour of your city. Provide maps and materials about the city's points of interests. Arrange for a driver and transportation to be available during your guest's stay, so that he or she can feel able to sightsee or enjoy other activities in safety and comfort.

When someone is far from home, evenings can be an especially lonely time. Unless your visitor prefers to spend the hours after work alone, plan some evening entertainment that you think he or she might enjoy. Unless you know your visitor's preferences well, it is best to offer a choice of options: an evening at the theater, a baseball game, or a concert, for example. If the guest is accompanied by a family member, plan activities that everyone can enjoy.

GIVING AND ACCEPTING GIFTS

SEVENTEEN

The right gift can speak volumes about your esteem for the recipient. So can the wrong one. Before giving, it's important to think carefully about company policy and tradition, the precise circumstances, the recipient, cost, and the nature of the gift.

COMPANY POLICY AND TRADITION

In certain cultures, gift-giving rituals are an important part of doing business. In the United States, each company has its own traditions and protocol for exchanging gifts. Procedures vary for different industries, as well as for individual corporations within an industry.

Some companies have very definite rules governing the giving and receiving of gifts. For instance, some companies view the giving of gifts by a vendor to be a form of bribery. Some set dollar limits on the value of gifts that employees may accept. In other companies, gift-giving parameters are governed largely by tradition. Before you present a gift, it's important that you know what is and is not appropriate, for the recipient's company as well as your own.

THE CIRCUMSTANCES

A gift can help express gratitude, congratulations, sympathy and holiday wishes. It can acknowledge personal or professional milestones (such as retirement or a 50th birthday). Again, consider the company's gift-giving policy and tradition before you give.

THE RECIPIENT

Your relationship with the recipient should be a major determining factor in your gift selection. Are you close personal friends, or simply business acquaintances? Is the recipient your boss, a client, a customer, or your assistant? The most appreciated gifts are ones that are selected specifically for the recipient, with his or her particular tastes or interests in mind.

THE COST

This can be a sticky issue. You don't want to be regarded as cheap, but neither do you want to be overly extravagant. Look to company policy or tradition for guidance. Always keep in mind that quality doesn't have to be exorbitantly expensive.

THE NATURE OF THE GIFT

If you know a little about the recipient, you may be able to select an appropriate gift that caters to his or her likes and interests. When in doubt, a gift of some favorite food or a gift certificate is usually welcome. You can always fall back on traditional business gifts like pens, pocket calendars and books. No matter how well you know the recipient or how good a sense of humor he or she has, tacky, suggestive or romantic gifts are never appropriate in a business setting.

When you receive a gift, be gracious. Even if you thank the giver in person, always follow up with a note. Include a specific positive statement about the gift. For example: "Thank you for your thoughtful gift. The pen is so beautiful that I keep it displayed on my desk."

There may be a time when you receive a gift that, for

one reason or another, must be returned. If the sender was clearly well-intentioned, be gracious and gentle, and offer a plausible explanation. If the cost of the gift exceeded the parameters set by your company, you might say, "It was very nice of you to think of me, but company policy will not allow me to accept this gift."

If a gift is obviously inappropriate or offensive, your refusal can be tactful and, at the same time, assertive: "The gift you sent to me is inappropriate. I am returning it to you." Whenever you return a gift, keep a copy of your note and a record of how you returned it (a postal receipt, for example) in your files.

BUSINESS ASSOCIATES WITH SPECIAL NEEDS

Until recently, many workplaces were not equipped to meet the needs of physically challenged employees. The lack of ramps, accessible restroom facilities, and other necessary accommodations kept many people with talent, skills, and desire from being able to become members of the workforce. However, 1992 saw the passage of the Americans with Disabilities Act. The law now requires businesses to make every reasonable effort to create environments where individuals with disabilities can function productively.

Many physically challenged workers can now participate more easily and effectively in the work environment. But there is still one barrier that, too often, remains: Many people who aren't physically challenged feel nervous or uncomfortable around people who are. In most cases, their discomfort or hesitancy is not a matter of rudeness. In fact, the truth is quite the opposite. Many people are afraid that they will offend someone who is physically challenged. They worry that they don't know the right things to say or do.

There is only one rule to remember when you interact with someone who is physically challenged:

• Focus on the person, not the disability.

Never assume that because a person has a disability, he or she can't communicate or doesn't want to interact. Nobody enjoys feeling isolated or ignored. All too often people with seeing, hearing, or other physical challenges are made to feel invisible. Here are some ways to prevent this from happening.

When you are introduced to a person with a disability, be prepared to shake hands. Note which hand the person offers, and respond in kind. A person with an artificial limb may offer his or her left hand instead of right. If a person is blind, ask, "Shall we shake hands?" Then touch your hand to his or hers.

When you approach someone with a visual impairment, immediately identify yourself. Be careful not to startle him or her with your sudden presence. Don't raise your voice. There is no reason to speak more loudly to someone who can't see. Never pet or interact with someone's guide dog without asking permission. The dog is working and shouldn't be distracted.

When you would like to initiate a conversation with a hearing impaired person, place yourself where he or she can see you easily. Wave, or gently tap the person on the shoulder. If he or she reads lips, be sure to speak slowly and form your words clearly. Always speak directly to hearing impaired people, even if there is an interpreter present. Stay well within his or her line of vision. Maintain eye contact with the person you are addressing, not with the interpreter. Don't use third-person references. Instead of asking a third person, "Would he (or she) like a cup of coffee," ask the person directly: "Would you like a cup of coffee?"

When you are speaking with someone who has difficulty talking, be patient and attentive. Listen carefully. Don't interrupt or try to be helpful by supplying words that are slow in coming. Let the person do his or her own talking. Then if you don't understand, say something. Repeat the part you do understand and allow him or her to continue.

118

If someone is in a wheelchair or motorized cart, do not assume that the person can't hear, see, or speak. To make conversation easier and more natural, lower yourself to his or her eye level.

Don't refer to someone as the "victim" of his or her disability. Don't refer to someone as "the blind person" or "a deaf mute." Most people with physical challenges resent being defined by their disabilities. Be sensitive and neutral in your descriptions. Instead of "handicap," use "disability." Instead of "blind person," try to think of someone as a person with a visual impairment.

If you are not sure whether to offer assistance to a physically challenged person, just ask. If the person needs help, instructions will be provided. If he or she says "no," respect his or her refusal. Never push the issue.

Basically, try to consider how you would wish to be treated and behave accordingly. People with disabilities are no more one-dimensional than anyone else. Like you, they are the sum of their thoughts, hopes, dreams and actions. They are not simply a symbol of their disability and don't want to be treated that way.

Here are some additional pointers for ensuring that you act properly with colleagues, clients and others who have disabilities.

- Never touch or lean on someone's wheelchair, unless given permission. It is seen as a part of the person.
- Don't assume that the person needs or wants your help — always ask first.
- Don't yell at hearing impaired people, and remember to look straight at them.

BECOMING A LEADER

People respect leaders. JFK. Abraham Lincoln. Golda Meir. Harriet Tubman. What are the specific traits that cause someone to become a great leader in business?

If becoming an effective, respected business leader is one of your lifetime goals, some of the points made in this book should help you in your quest. There are several identifiable and memorable traits that all great leaders seem to share. Here are some.

A GREAT LEADER:

- **Gets along with others.** This is one of the golden rules of business. Many times people wonder how someone who may not have had the best credentials managed to get himself or herself promoted. It is not always a result of how much you know, sometimes it is how well you get along with everyone. The candidate who got to the top is likely to be someone who knows how to get along with everyone in the company, from the cleaning crew to the president.

- **Is prepared for the worst and stays calm.** Murphy's law has taught us all that if something can go wrong, it will. This includes business meetings, presentations to new clients, or anything else that is your responsibility in the workplace.

- **Makes clients or colleagues feel comfortable by using small talk.** This may sound relatively insignificant, but there is nothing more awkward and unnerving than silence. This is an art that is easily practiced with friends, family or the mail carrier.

- **Doesn't keep people waiting and isn't late.** Making someone wait is one way to guarantee getting off on the wrong foot.

- **Is respectful of other people's time.** Related to not being late, this trait precludes other insensitive behaviors as well. In today's competitive environment, stopping to chitchat when your colleague is under the gun, interrupting people, barging into someone's office, or wasting someone's time in a poorly planned meeting are all good examples of serious business faux pas.

- **Respects another person's space.** It is rude to place a briefcase on someone's table or desk, to use someone's telephone or computer without permission, or to peek at the papers on the desk while waiting for a meeting to begin.

- **Has excellent listening skills.** Being a good listener is crucial to becoming successful. It is a mistake to interrupt or monopolize a conversation. Asking questions is fine.

- **Dresses appropriately.** Good grooming is necessary for making a professional impression.

- **Returns phone calls.** This is simply a reflection of respect for the other person.

It would be wonderful if learning and following a single set of important guidelines could guarantee that you would join the ranks of great leaders. It can't, of course, because a great leader is something more than the sum of certain essential and wonderful traits. But keeping these guidelines in mind can't hurt. Even if following them does not ultimately help you to become a great business leader, it will help you to become a consummate professional, with the respect and admiration of your peers.

**"Alright, men ... I mean,
ladies and gentlemen ... I mean,
esteemed colleagues, follow me!"**

INDEX

INDEX

INDEX

INDEX

INDEX

INDEX

About Marjorie Brody, MA, CSP, CMC
Motivational speaker, executive coach, seminar leader

Marjorie Brody, MA, CSP, CMC, one of "Pennsylvania's 1999 Best 50 Women in Business," is the founder and president of Brody Communications Ltd. She wears four hats: company president, professional speaker, trainer/executive coach, and published author.

In her role as president, Marjorie has taken her vision of how presentation and business communication skills could best be taught, and developed customized programs for a range of corporations and individuals.

As an internationally recognized speaker, Marjorie proudly wears the designation of CSP — Certified Speaking Professional — so designated by the National Speakers Association. She is the ninth person with a CSP to also hold the title of CMC — Certified Management Consultant — awarded by the Institute of Management Consultants. Marjorie was one of 12 women selected as "1999 Distinguished National Leaders" by the National Association of Women Business Owners, Greater Philadelphia Chapter. She was also one of 25 women selected as "1999 Women of Distinction" by the *Philadelphia Business Journal*, National Association of Women Business Owners and The Forum of Executive Women.

Marjorie is regularly contacted by members of the national media for her expert commentary on a variety of workplace and career issues. She has appeared on CNBC, Fox-TV News and in *The Wall Street Journal*, *USA Today*, *The Washington Post*, *BusinessWeek*, *People*, *Fortune*, *Glamour*, *Good Housekeeping* and many more publications. She is also a member of the editorial board at *communication briefings* newsletter.

131

Her topics include business etiquette, presentation skills, building your business, effective self-marketing strategies, and how people can turn their career dreams into reality. Marjorie travels extensively as a trainer/executive coach, sharing her knowledge with people in the U.S. and abroad, conducting seminars/workshops on presentation skills, business etiquette, personal marketing, and networking. Through repeat business and referrals, she has built up an impressive client roster of *Fortune* 100 and 500 companies. Some clients include: EDS, Lockheed Martin, Merck & Co., Microsoft Corp., Pfizer Inc., PricewaterhouseCoopers, SAP America, Inc., Glaxo SmithKline and Visa International.

A well-published writer and author, Marjorie Brody has authored 15 books, including the four-booklet series *21st Century Pocket Guides to Proper Business Protocol* (Career Skills Press) and *Speaking Is An Audience-Centered Sport* (Career Skills Press). Marjorie has six audio cassette programs, including: "21 Common Mistakes for 21st Century Etiquette & How Not To Make Them" and "Sell Yourself ... You Are the Product." Marjorie also has a video, "Present Like a Pro." The newest Brody Communications Ltd. learning resource is Web-based Internet training that features her business etiquette expertise. Marjorie is profiled on several speaking- and training-related sites on the World Wide Web, and has two home pages: www.BrodyCommunications.com and www.marjoriebrody.com.

Marjorie is a Professor Emeritus at Bucks County Community College, immediate past president of Liberty Bell Speakers Association (LBSA), a member of the National Speakers Association, Institute of Management Consultants, American Society for Training and Development, National Association for Female Executives, The Forum of Executive Women, National Association of Women Business Owners, and is a founding member of Master Speakers International, and an affiliate member of the International Association for Continuing Education and Training. She is also a founding professor of MentorU.com, and a board member of Mentoring Partnerships, Inc. and Women's Business Development Center. Marjorie was LBSA "Chapter Member of the Year" in 1997 and LBSA's "Speaker of the Year" in 1999.

About Brody Communications Ltd.

The ability to connect & communicate effectively is essential for both individual and corporate success. Our mission is to provide our clients with the tools and skills needed to reach their full potential.

Presentation Skills

Training Programs

- **Present With Success**
- **Powerful Presentation Skills**
- **Persuasive Speaking**
- **Advanced Presentation Skills**
- **Powerful Presentation Skills for Sales Professionals**
- **Powerful Presentation Skills for Technical Professionals**
- **Team Presentations**
- **The Power of Everyday Presentation & Facilitation**
- **Speaking to Lead & Inspire**
- **Make Your Point in a Heartbeat**
- **Presenting in a Wired World**

Coaching

- **Presentation skills**
- **Voice & Diction**
- **Dealing With The Media**

Keynote Presentations

- **Present Like a Pro**

Business Communications

Training Programs

- **The Art of Listening**
- **Interpersonal Communication Skills**
- **Maximizing Customer Satisfaction**
- **Telephoning With Confidence**
- **Managing Conflict**
- **Assertive Communications**
- **Negotiating for Agreement**
- **Collaborative Win-Win Negotiation Skills**
- **Understanding Behavior Using Myers-Briggs**
- **Meetings That Work**
- **Dealing With Difficult People**
- **Improving Organizational Communication**
- **Business Writing**
  - Effective Business Writing
  - Writing For Results
  - Effective Proposal Writing
  - Business Writing For the Technical Professional
  - Grammar Brush-Up
  - Proofreading & Editing Techniques
- **Training Techniques**
  - Effective On-the-Job Training
  - Facilitator Training
  - Train the Trainer

Coaching

- **The Dynamic Professional**
- **Executive Presence**
- **Interpersonal Communications**
- **360 Degree Feedback**
- **Myers-Briggs**

Organizational Development Consulting

Keynote Presentations

- **Have You Ever ... ? (Etiquette Faux Pas That Can Cost a Career)**
- **Present Like a Pro**
- **Increase Possibilities: Perfect Your Presence**

Strategies to Advance Careers

Training Programs

- **Business Etiquette Excellence**
- **Professional Presence**
- **Networking Know-How**
- **Market Your MAGIC**
- **Enhancing Personal Effectiveness**
- **Life Management — Achieving Balance in Your Personal & Professional Life**
- **Personal Goal Setting**
- **Stress — Making it Work For You**
- **Time Management**
- **Working for More Than One Boss**
- **Managing Change**
- **Influencing Others**
- **Problem Solving & Decision Making**
- **Working Smarter Not Harder**
- **Assertive Communication Skills**

Coaching

- **The Dynamic Professional**
- **Executive Excellence**
- **Image Consulting**

- Voice & Dictation
- Interpersonal Communications
- Performance Improvement
- 360 Degree Feedback

Keynote Presentations

- Have You Ever ... ? (Etiquette Faux Pas That Can Cost a Career)
- Present Like a Pro
- Increase Possibilities: Perfect Your Presence
- When Dreaming is Not Enough ...
- Market Your MAGIC

Management Development

Training Programs

- Building and Managing Effective Working Relationships
- Coaching for Peak Performance
- Project Management
- Motivating Employees
- Managers as Leaders
- How to Manage Successfully in a Changing Workplace
- Teams
    Enhancing Team Communications
    From Lead Worker to Team Leader
    Facilitating Effective Team Meetings
    Building Effective Work Teams

Coaching

- The Dynamic Professional

- Executive Presence
- Interpersonal Communications
- 360 Degree Feedback
- Myers-Briggs
- Performance Improvement

Skills for Sales Professionals

Training Programs

- Coaching and Sales Presentations for Sales Managers
- Make Your Point in a Heartbeat
- The Power of Everyday Presentations & Facilitation

Coaching

Customized one-on-one for all salespeople whose potential can be maximized by individual attention.

Keynote Presentations

- Have You Ever ... ? (Etiquette Faux Pas That Can Cost a Career)
- Present Like a Pro
- Increase Possibilities: Perfect Your Presence
- When Dreaming is Not Enough ...
- Market Your MAGIC

Communicating Internationally

Training Programs

- American Etiquette for International

Employees
- **International Awareness**
- **Intercultural Communications: Building Effective Global Working Relationships**
- **Intensive English Course for Foreign-Born Professionals**

Keynote Presentations

- **Business Rules (American Etiquette for International Employees)**

Executive Excellence

A specialized team of Brody Communications training and coaching professionals deliver a wide range of programs created specifically for top-level executives and fast-trackers. Emphasis is on individual development.

- Executive coaching for presentations — one-on-one coaching allows for hands-on, specific feedback. Each session is videotaped and critiqued.
- Professional presence in and out of the boardroom
- Leadership skills tune up
- Media readiness
- Skillful business entertaining — includes managing business/social events
- Executive negotiation strategies

Learning Tools by Marjorie Brody, MA, CSP, CMC

Books

1) *New!* 21st Century Pocket Guides to Proper
    Business Protocol (Career Skills Press) $28.00
    Rules For the Wired (part one of four)
    Creating First Impressions That Can Lead to Lasting
    Impressions (part two of four)
    Make the Work Environment Work For You (part three
    of four)
    Have Office, Will Travel: Doing Business in Social
    Settings and on the Road (part four of four)
    — Series comes with free bookmark! —

Ettiquette Bundle — $35

Four-booklet series: "21st Century Pocket Guides to
Proper Business Protocol"

"21 Common Mistakes for 21st Century Etiquette &
How Not To Make Them" (tape)

"21 Guidelines for 21st Century Business Protocol"
(bookmark)

---

2) Speaking is an Audience-Centered Sport (Career
    Skills Press $19.95
3) Speaking Your Way to the Top: Making Powerful
    Business Presentations (Allyn & Bacon) $12.00
4) Complete Business Etiquette Handbook
    (Prentice Hall) $29.95
5) 21 Ways to Springboard Your Speaking, Training
    & Consulting Career (Career Skills Press) $14.95
6) *New!* Power Marketing for Consultants ...